ABOVE & BELOW:
THE UNOFFICIAL 25TH ANNIVERSARY
BEAUTY
AND THE
BEAST
COMPANION *by Edward Gross*

Published in the USA by:
BearManor Media
PO Box 1129
Duncan, Oklahoma 73534-1129
www.bearmanormedia.com

ISBN 978-1-59393-280-0

Printed in the United States of America.
Book design by Brian Pearce | Red Jacket Press.

TABLE OF CONTENTS

AN INTRODUCTION

It's somewhat frightening to consider how quickly 25 years can pass. Can it *really* be that long since CBS debuted *Beauty and the Beast*, a show that managed to touch the hearts and imagination for a generation whose love for it — and the eternal love the series itself represents — still burns brightly?

In my mind, *B&B* never really went away. That point drove itself home to me back in the fall of 2007 when I found myself drawn to the series *Moonlight*, which stars Alex O'Loughlin as private eye Mick St. John, who also happens to be a vampire; and Sophia Myles as Internet news reporter Beth Turner. The series chronicles their seemingly fated yet unconsummated relationship as they help people from both their worlds.

Sounds downright *Beauty and the Beast*, doesn't it?

The attraction of *Moonlight* for me was on several levels, the first being that I've always been a sucker (bad pun definitely intended) for the vampire genre. Second, the series is co-created by Ron Koslow, someone I'd known for over two decades, so where he goes, I follow. Third, *Moonlight*'s premiere was almost 20 years to the day that the same network (CBS) debuted Ron's "other" TV series, the aforementioned *Beauty and the Beast*, a modern day version of the classic fairy tale starring Linda Hamilton and Ron Perlman, and a show that I was fairly obsessed with when it debuted.

Back in the late 1980s and early 1990s, I had written or edited several volumes devoted to *Beauty and the Beast*. Doing so allowed me to accomplish one feat that I was particularly proud of: the show's entire writing staff and several if its most prominent directors took the time to be interviewed about all 56 episodes of the series. In retrospect, those interview sessions have resulted in an unprecedented historical look back at the series, tracing it from the excitement surrounding its early development through the challenges of remaining true to Ron Koslow's concept while dealing with network interference, being forced to adjust to rising or declining ratings and, most importantly, having to reconfigure the show for its third season after Linda Hamilton announced that she was leaving.

Above & Below: The Unofficial 25th Anniversary Beauty and the Beast Companion — which, ideally, should be read while watching episodes of the show on DVD — is a complete behind-the-scenes look at the making of the show episode-by episode, season-by-season, and as such hopefully captures some of the magic that the series did. For me, editing and updating this material was an opportunity to revisit my past, and whether you're a veteran fan or a newcomer, I hope you'll enjoy the journey to follow.

Edward Gross
May, 2012

FROM LEFT TO RIGHT ARE RON PERLMAN AS VINCENT, ROY DOTRICE AS FATHER AND LINDA HAMILTON AS CATHERINE.

CREATING
TWO WORLDS

Like many fairy tales, the original story of *Beauty and the Beast* was rather simplistic on a surface level, essentially reinforcing the adage that you can't judge a book by its cover. To wit, we have a princess who falls in love with a lion-man, a mutant to be sure, and yet a being who possesses more humanity than any man she has ever met. Their love is an unrequited one, until the moment when beauty kisses the beast, effectively transforming him into a prince and allowing them to live happily ever after. Nice and simple, right? Yet it's a timeless story, filled with romance and hope, and at least part of the reason that the 1987-90 live action CBS series enjoys such a cult success.

As a press release for the show states, "The original fable is part of a cycle of transformation myths, including such classics as *The Frog Prince*, in which the 'ugly being,' when accepted and shown love, is transformed into something beautiful. These myths are meant to instruct our culture on the transforming power of love and the wisdom of prizing inner beauty and truth."

Beauty and the Beast was put on film in the 1946 classic Jean Cocteau film of the same name and, of course, the 1991 Disney animated version, which in itself spawned the long-running stage musical. Both versions were period pieces, in true fairy tale settings, and it wasn't until writer/producer Ron Koslow studied the idea that its basic principles were applied to a modern setting.

"What we've tried to do is create a compelling, contemporary version of the original story, centering on a new mythic figure — an interesting kind of urban hero," Koslow explained. "We also wanted to tell a classical love story in a contemporary context. *Beauty and the Beast* affords us the opportunity to do just that, given the insurmountable obstacles which stand in the way of a complete relationship between Vincent and Catherine. We now have a chance to explore this kind of romance on television, with all its impossibility and longing."

The premise of the series is unique: Assistant District Attorney Catherine Chandler who, because of a case of mistaken identity, is attacked by a group of punks who slash up her face and leave her for dead in Central Park. Her body is found by Vincent, the Beast, who takes her beneath the streets of New York to a wondrous underworld beyond imagination which is led by a man known as Father, and populated by people who have migrated from the surface. There she heals, her face wrapped in bandages and her only solace coming from the soothing voice of Vincent. The healing process is slow, and the two of them gradually fall in love. Then Catherine removes the bandages and discovers what Vincent truly is. Yet as was the case with her predecessors involved in this tale, her love remains, albeit in an unconsummated form.

The television version of *Beauty and the Beast* owes its existence to the desire of former CBS Entertainment President Kim LeMasters, who was curious to see if the classic fairy tale could somehow be updated in such a way that it could appeal to audiences of the time. The challenge, naturally, was to find someone capable of translating this idea into a premise that would connect with television viewers. Reportedly he went to numerous producers, including Kenneth Johnson ("*V,*" *Alien Nation*), but eventually struck gold with motion picture writer/producer Koslow.

Koslow, whose screen credits included *First Born* and *Into the Night*, and who most recently co-created and executive produced CBS' vampire P.I. series *Moonlight*, came up with a concept that would juxtapose the classic fairy tale upon a modern setting.

Said Koslow at the time of the show's debut in 1987, "The relationship between Catherine and Vincent will be continually challenged by the fact that Vincent will remain who he is — a perfect man; ironically, Catherine's perfect soul mate — trapped in an imperfect body. The power of his character lies in the fact that he's a survivor who accepts who he is, and continues to move forward."

Offers producer Howard Gordon, whose subsequent credits include *The X-Files, Buffy the Vampire Slayer, 24, Homeland* and *Awake*, but who began on the show as a story editor, "This show has a kind of romance that harkened back to a former age. It just appeals on a real visceral level, the fact that there was this really deep romance, and he was this creature who was a hero for our time. A new hero, basically. The tone of the show is really two-tier. We really wanted to portray the above world as realistically as possible. Even if almost stylized, we wanted to emphasize the grittiness, speed and fast pace in counterpoint to the real lyrical, soft-toned underworld. So on a broad thematic level, that's what we were trying to do. We were making every effort to keep this show unique. We didn't want it to be 'Starsky and the Beast.'"

The modern setting of the series, particularly the underground world, was inspired, according to Koslow, by an article he had read several years earlier which described people who were living in the steam tunnels below the Waldorf Astoria in Manhattan, who were getting their food from the dumpsters behind the hotel restaurant and generally living off of what was disposed of by the world above them. Further research revealed to him that there were more than 300 miles of tunnels beneath the city. The original purpose of these tunnels was to serve as conduits for steam, water and electricity, but the majority of these, built over a century ago, remain unexplored because the maps which hold the key to their locations have been long lost. There are also, as he discovered, underground caverns and rivers beneath Manhattan Island. All of this together inspired the world of Vincent and the others who live underground.

"Since then," Koslow said, "I have wanted to do a show which could incorporate the various textures of New York City, from the Upper East Side to the halls of power, the public institutions and, finally, this whole subterranean secret world below the streets. And what we're postulating in the show is a sort of utopian answer to the world above. Father is the leader of society, and Vincent is poised to take over. They're made up of a secret circle of healers who find people in transition. And then, there are those who have rejected the values of the world above."

The final ingredient of *Beauty and the Beast* television series that separates it from all other incarnations of the fable, is that Catherine's job as a lawyer involves her in different situations on the surface, which manage to become intertwined with Vincent's. In addition, as the first season developed, the stories began to alternate between those having to do with people on the surface and those who reside in the underworld.

Director Paul Lynch, who at the time he directed episodes of *Beauty and the Beast* was also directing episodes of *Star Trek: The Next Generation* and *The New Twilight Zone*, expressed the enthusiasm he felt for the series even *before* it ever went on the air. Interestingly, much of what he says held true throughout the first season.

"It's quite interesting and I think it's going to work," he said. "It's a family-oriented show so there isn't a lot of violence. It's mostly human drama storytelling, and that's what I'm hoping will hold it together, because they are good human stories. One that I did was about old folks being evicted from their apartments ('Terrible Savior'), and how wrong that is. They seem to all be strong scripts, which was the same with *The Twilight Zone*. Do you remember *East Side/West Side*? It was with George C. Scott as a welfare worker in New York City, and the stories are very similar to the ones they did back then. They're not black and white stories, but they're stories about people with problems in today's world, and the DA gets involved in trying to solve the situation, and to help finish solving it is Perlman as Vincent. If you have a good script, you're 95% there.

"It's difficult," he added, "because of the way that television has changed over the years. Up until the late 1960s television was, for the most part, very intelligent, along the lines of *Playhouse 90, Climax* and so on. Good dramatic stories, and that's all they had. As the medium broadened its base, it sort of got away from serious television and I think it's been going that way ever since. I think *Beauty and the Beast* is the kind of show that can at least help to reverse that trend."

And thus *Beauty and the Beast* was born, with Linda Hamilton (who had made great impact as Sarah Connor in James Cameron's *The Terminator* and not as great an impact in the godawful *King Kong Lives*) being signed to portray Catherine. Cast opposite her was Ron Perlman, whose credits at the time included make-up intensive roles in *Quest For Fire* and *Name of the Rose*, and who is more recently scoring as *Hellboy* and on television in *Sons of Anarchy*. Like Hamilton, he wasn't looking for a TV role and, particularly, one that required a great deal of make-up. But the approach to the material and the make-up designed by Rick Baker convinced him otherwise.

The late director Richard Franklin, whose credits include the thrillers *Psycho II, Cloak and Dagger, Link, F/X 2: The Art of Illusion* and the pilot episode of *Beauty and the Beast*, admitted at the time that there was a challenge in sustaining a show like *B&B*.

"The difficulty," he said, "I think they're going to have is that *Beauty and the Beast* is a fantasy that sustains through to a transformation. That is, the Beast turning into a prince. Now the longer the show goes on, the longer they're holding back on that transformation. I'm not saying there are plans to ever have him transforming into a prince so that everything turns out happily. The difficulty in doing the show week after week is that he can't turn into a prince at the end, so the stories are always kind of open-ended and the relationship between *Beauty and the Beast* is not moving towards a conclusion in the same way that it does in the original."

"That was certainly a question, and it was one question I posed to Koslow when he first called me," explains author George R.R. Martin (represented on television by HBO's *Game of Thrones*, based on his series of fantasy novels). "I could see from the pilot that there were ways to go that I thought were very interesting, and there were ways to go that were not very interesting. I think that there were certain elements from the network right at the beginning that regarded us as a hairy version of *The Hulk*, with the obligatory rescue at the end of the fourth act and that kind of thing. If we were going to be primarily an action/adventure show oriented toward children with an obligatory beast-out at the end of the second act, and a major rescue at the end of the fourth act, I really didn't want to be involved with it. But from talking to Ron, it became clear that his ambitions for the show were very high and that he regarded it as adult-oriented drama, rather that formula action/adventure. That was one of the factors that changed my mind, and determined that I would take a crack at it. Then, once we were out there, determining which way to go was part of the challenge.

"There were various stages in the development of the show," he adds. "Early on, of course, the network was kind of putting us precisely in the direction we didn't want to go: formula action/adventure kind of scripts. They were putting restrictions on us in the first season which we labored under that were kind of difficult, including the most irritating to me: they didn't want to see any other people in the underworld. Initially, the network saw it as a cop show with a hairy hero who saved people at the end. I think there were always elements at the network that thought the tunnel people were kind of strange and didn't quite know what to make of them. Of course from my background, the tunnel people were precisely the elements that interested me the most: that whole tunnel society, and the world down there, Vincent and his origins...the fantastic elements. Thankfully, we were finally able to break through when the ratings were strong enough and we earned a little freedom to do what we wanted. These battles are worth fighting, because sometimes you lose them for a while, but eventually the tide turns. In our case, that turn came in the middle of the first season with 'An Impossible Silence' and 'Shades of Grey,' in which we were finally able to introduce the underground community in the way we wanted to."

Alex Gansa, whose producing credits most recently include *Wolf Lake*, *Numbers* and *Homecoming*, adds that he and writing partner Howard Gordon love the pilot for the series. "Compared to the other dreck we had been seeing in reference to work possibilities, it was amazing and incredibly different. At the same time, we didn't know what we were going to do with it. Since *Beauty and the Beast* was transformation myth, and there was a transformation at the end of the pilot in that she accepted him, it became very difficult to know where the show would go from there. There were a lot of questions about the kind of longevity the show would enjoy. Ideally, I think *Beauty and the Beast* should have run for eight or nine episodes and told a very coherent story. As is the nature of television, we had to stretch it out and it just became too much. We would hear freelance writers come in with ideas, and the dearth of good ideas was just astounding. So we were all banging our heads against the wall, trying to come up with stories. Also, at that point it becomes a marathon. After a while it becomes a struggle for mediocrity, and that struggle's not a very fruitful one, personally or professionally."

For Gansa, the most exciting aspect of the show was developing its direction following the pilot. "That was the best time, because nobody had any idea what we were going to do, nobody knew what to expect," he says. "It was the most excitingly creative time I've had in Hollywood, only because the show could have gone in any number of directions, most of which would have been horrible. The way it evolved was very exciting."

FOR LINDA HAMILTON, WHO PLAYS CATHERINE CHANDLER, THE LACK OF CHARACTER PROGRESSION ON THE SHOW GREW TIRESOME (PHOTO: CBS).

REFLECTIONS
OF BEAUTY

During the early days of *Beauty and the Beast*'s run, Linda Hamilton was interviewed about the series and her role of Catherine Chandler. Interestingly, her enthusiasm *then* for the part and the show was markedly different than it's been more recently when asked about it.

"The role was written for me," she explained in the late 1980s. "Ron Koslow wrote it specifically for me. A lot of people see me in this kind of role from the film *Terminator*. Because in the pilot especially it starts out with Catherine being weak and she grows and transforms and gets in touch with her courage. That is what I did in the *Terminator* role also. So that kind of role, once you've done it, it's like, 'Oh, Linda Hamilton can do that, because I've seen her do that.' That's the way you get a lot of parts.

"They approached me a lot," she added. "Not me personally, but my agent. He said he had a series and I put my foot down and said, 'Absolutely not.' I don't know how it happened. I still don't know. They finally beat down my door. Finally, my agent had a meeting with them. He walked out of that room saying I would want to do this role. He really loved the role. So he called me and said he had this role that I should look at. I read it and told him, 'Let me think about this.' Then I went to the meeting and it happened."

Part of the reason she said yes was Ron Perlman as Vincent. "I had seen a drawing of him," Hamilton explained. "That was one of the selling points of the meeting, because it was very well done. You know, these things make or break a show. I saw this diagram of Vincent that Rick Baker had drawn up and I just went, 'Wow!' Then when I saw him, I just thought he was extraordinary looking. My feelings changed. I mean, he transforms you. Not that he's not a pretty terrific person without makeup, but something extraordinary happens to him, and I find him extraordinarily attractive."

As to why the character of Vincent struck such a chord with people, she smiled, "Because he *is* sexy. Because he's a Renaissance man. I mean, he reads me Shakespeare sonnets. He really is just a true, noble, generous man; with no actually silly-little-life demands that most people place on each other. It just goes much further than that."

In terms of establishing who Catherine was as a person, she noted, "I built Catherine on parts of myself, parts that might not always be in play, but parts that are there nevertheless. The part that I would say is least like me is her constant doubting of herself. Is she strong enough, is she this or that? That's tough. I find that kind of dialogue very tough to play. They've actually taken my character away from that a little bit. It's not that I don't have any vulnerabilities, but I find her constant harping on them very frustrating. Obviously I have my places of fear, great fear, great vulnerabilities, but I don't parade them."

Hamilton left the show following its second season, which she felt was more than enough as expressed in more recent interviews. "Skip the '80s!" she told *Den of Geek.com*. "*Beauty and the Beast* was in the '80s, I left in '89 and *Beauty and the Beast* was very definitive for me, because it was several years of my life and really hard. Fifteen hours a day and you know [now] we're used to doing it or three months and then having a break, but this is nine months and when you're off you just want to lie down for three months. It's really aging; it's hard!"

"It made a big impact," she added to *Terminator Files.com*, "and I don't regret it. I look back on it very lovingly now. Two years was the perfect amount of time. I would not have been happy had I continued. My pregnancy was the genuine reason I decided to leave when I did. It served me well and I adored many of the show's elements, but I would have no interest in playing Catherine again. Television is a frustrating medium to be involved in as characters aren't evolved, they're endlessly repeated. I really wanted my relationship with Ron Perlman to move along and investigate those interesting facets. It never happened nor was it going to. Apparently the third season got much darker after I'd left, but I never saw it."

Assignment X.com asked her if somebody came along with the idea of a theatrical film, would she find that intriguing? "The fans will never give up on that idea, even though at this point I would feel like a geriatric Catherine Chandler," she laughed. "But that's what makes fans great: they're blind to your flaws. They're blind to the fact you are aging. The fans definitely like the idea, but no one else has thought of going on with that."

In that same interview, she said that she had actually gone to a *Beauty and the Beast* convention in recent years and noted that the fan community is continually getting smaller. "The message of love and compassion and art is what I think enflames the fans as much as the love story," she mused. "Those fans are amazingly loyal, but right now there's several generations that never saw it. My own children at 18 and 21 are sophisticated in a way that I couldn't even show them *Beauty and the Beast*, because they've seen so many shows like *24* — shows that are so sophisticated and smart that they would laugh me out of the house. It was *so* '80s. I haven't seen it since I left it, but I have the box set, so some day..."

"IT WAS A GREAT LEARNING PROCESS," SAID LINDA HAMILTON EARLY
ON, "AND EMPOWERING TO BE THE STAR OF A SERIES." (PHOTO: CBS).

THERE WAS NO IDENTITY CRISIS FOR RON PERLMAN WHEN HE PLAYED
HIS BEAUTY AND THE BEAST ALTER EGO. "I THINK VINCENT *IS* THE
PRINCE," HE SAYS.

THE BEAST'S
POINT OF VIEW

Back during the show's first season, the author had an opportunity to talk to Ron Perlman, who reflected on the role and the show in general.

"I think Vincent *is* the Prince," he said, "and I think the job that Rick Baker has done, and the job that the writers have done and the job that I'm trying to do, bears that out in every episode. He is the most sublime thing in Catherine Chandler's life. He doesn't need to change — to become the prince — to be accepted by her. That's how we get around the transformation part of the story. There's no reason to see this guy change, because he's as close to perfect as you're going to get. There's a lot to be said for people who ask, 'How the hell are we going to sustain this for 22 weeks a year for the next five years?' That's the exercise, and every week we address that exercise with various degrees of success. We've already put some wonderful episodes on the air, and as long as we can do that, and as long as the writers stay as fertile as they've been, then the question will be answered as we go along."

Perlman is speaking of the final moments of the original tale of *Beauty and the Beast*, as well as the classic Cocteau film of the same name. As to the show's appeal, he offered, "It's *so* romantic, and it's not really very science fiction or fantasy oriented. It's very real. They've found very contemporary equivalents to the magical and fanciful elements, certainly, but in a very real setting. It's real easy to suspend your disbelief, which is one of the things that I have discovered working on it. The benefits of playing Vincent are incredible. There are elements that one has to come to grips with in terms of Vincent's character, which are so elevated, noble and regal, you can't help but get involved. He's so spiritual, so sensitive to the world and humanity around him, that I've begun look at the world through his eyes, because I spend so many hours of my day walking in his shoes.

"I'm not going to say that I become Vincent," he clarified. "I don't want you to interpret this in that way, but the only thing an actor has as his tools is his own experience, and you have to find things in you to play that the character in the script calls for. Insofar as I've been doing that to the degree I have been, yes, I've become very intimately involved in what I have in me that's similar to Vincent. One of the turn-ons of being an actor is being given the opportunity to occasionally be more than you are, or less than you are. It certainly takes you out of the realm of being yourself."

Perlman, who has seemingly made a career for himself as an actor who dons prosthetics, feels that there is a significant difference between Vincent and some of his earlier roles in such films as *Quest For Fire* and *The Name of the Rose*, in which he portrayed, respectively, a prehistoric caveman and a disfigured monk.

"The humanity of those two people was so abstract that I had to form a new level of behavior," he explained. "A new walk, a new voice, a new language, new places that the language comes from...those are all intellectual decisions and inventive decisions. Vincent needs to be played right from the heart. What state his emotions are in at any given moment dictates how he is to be played. Not invention, not imagination or any of those things. Just purely using the scripts as a guideline to what is needed emotionally in a given situation. It's a different type of acting than I've ever had to do. I'm really enjoying it, because it's very honest and simple; it's the kind of thing I've been hoping for. I play both now, and Vincent, aside from the fact that he is so physically different, is definitely a romantic hero."

Indeed, Vincent's romantic appeal was registered all across the country, with women of all ages finding themselves drawn to his nobility of spirit. In fact, as much as was the case with the character of *Star Trek*'s Mr. Spock, the physical and emotional differences between Vincent and everyone else had led to a large degree of fantasy among the show's distaff fans. Many of them forwarded suggestive letters to the actor. But what is the appeal?

"First of all," responded Perlman, "there's not a character around that I've come into contact with who possesses as much humility as he does. That humility serves as a backdrop to his other qualities, which are incredible strength, both spiritual and physical and an innate leadership quality based on his solitude and aloneness and good judgment, as well as his compassion for the underdog. Those who have been dealt a few cards less in the big deal. Certainly he has been, and his compassion makes him a sort of Albert Sweitzer. He's achieved a sort of self-actualization in his own life and he's very, very secure in what he is and who he is. In fact, he's so secure that he is able to begin to live for the world around him rather than for himself. A character like that is very rare in life. There are those people out there, but they're usually Nobel Peace Prize winners. Those are the things I see in Vincent, and those are the things I try to put into the playing of him that people are responding to."

Perlman himself responded immediately to the role. He had appeared in a number of feature films and stage productions, and attained perhaps the most attention for his role in *The Name of the Rose*, which, he feels, was indirectly responsible for his being cast as Vincent.

PRIOR TO *SONS OF ANARCHY*, RON PERLMAN OFTEN PLAYED ROLES THAT REQUIRED PROSTHETICS, WHETHER IT WAS *QUEST FOR FIRE, NAME OF THE ROSE, HELLBOY* OR, OF COURSE, *BEAUTY AND THE BEAST* (PHOTO: CBS).

"My version of it is probably a lot different from other people's versions," Perlman laughed, "but at the time they were conceptualizing this series, *The Name of the Rose* had been released. 20th Century Fox, the film's distributor, mounted a modest Oscar nomination campaign on my behalf, so I was very prominent in the press and I got real good reviews for the performance. I guess my name went on that list of guys who do well in prosthetics,

VINCENT POSSESSED A NOBILITY OF SPIRIT THAT APPEALED TO RON PERLMAN AND THE SHOW'S MILLIONS OF FANS (PHOTO: CBS).

and they submitted my name to the show. Rick Baker, who was designing Vincent's makeup, went heavily to bat for me, because he knew the films I had been in and knew that I would be used to the battle that would have to be fought in getting the makeup on every day. Then I went in and read, and my empathy for the character and the script was, I guess, apparent and from what I understand, I really didn't have much competition once I read. When I went to read for the network, I had only read the script twice because I didn't want to mess with it. Usually you spend weeks getting into a character, but with Vincent I just wanted to leave an extension of my first instinct of what he was, because that was so clear to me. It was an immediate response, which is how fleshed out I thought the character was in the script, which is really a tribute to Ron Koslow's writing.

"I had played beasts prior to this, but this was not only a beast, but a beast who lived as an extension of his pain every moment of every day. All of that was there in the relationship with this woman who opened up all of these new feelings in him. It was just mind-blowing that somebody could come up with a character that crystallized all of the beasts that had ever been written in history, including the Hunchback of Notre Dame, the beast from the Cocteau film and the beast that I played in *Name of the Rose*. These guys, I always felt, had tremendous feelings underneath their ugliness and those things were always touched on by the other characterizations, but never as articulately or as fleshed out as in this version. I saw an incredible sensitivity on the part of the writer for this man's pain, and yet his ability to transcend that pain."

Despite prior statements to the contrary, Perlman ultimately decided to go ahead with yet another role which required a heavy amount of make-up, but this was different from all the others in that it became a daily and sometimes grueling experience. And yet that aspect of playing Vincent didn't seem to bother him, as the benefits of playing the character were stronger than any of the drawbacks.

"Make-up has always been rather freeing for me," Perlman admits. "When you're playing a character, you're playing someone other than yourself, and when you physically put something on that makes you look like somebody else, then it frees you to be that person, rather than being encumbered by the limitations of what you look like. It is, however, something of a nuisance to be sitting in a chair four hours every day to get made up, and then for an hour to get the makeup taken off. So that's five hours added on to whatever kind of shooting day we have, and that's been averaging about 12 or 14 hours. I have had more than my fair share of 20-hour days. Now that we have been doing this for quite a while, it's been a real test of my endurance. So far the incredible excitement I have for just getting to play this character who's so much larger than life, so incredible, far outweigh the negatives. It's the most beautiful character I've ever played, and maybe that I ever will. He's a combination of Hamlet, Superman and the Cocteau beast. Maybe I never will get tired of it, no matter what the problems are."

As previously noted, the thrust behind *Beauty and the Beast* is the Vincent/Catherine romance, and as one watches the on-screen sparks between the two characters, the question of what the Perlman/Hamilton relationship is like arises. As does the inevitable inquiry as to when the on-screen duo will consummate their relationship, if ever.

"I truly believe the chemistry between Linda and myself is very strong," Perlman says. "My respect for her as an actress is higher than that I have for anyone I've ever worked with. She's terrific, a hard worker, incredibly well disciplined and incredibly respectful of the art and the material, and we get along real well. We find no difficulty in playing those scenes with each other, although we've never talked about it. I guess neither of us wants to talk about it, because there's a spirituality between them that remains unspoken between Linda Hamilton and Ron Perlman. We just do it. We don't question it and we don't think about it too much. There's that level of trust, which I tip my hat to.

"In terms of the consummation of the relationship, we're already getting that question from people. The press hasn't jumped on it yet, but I'm sure they will. I think there's a tremendous amount of heat between these two characters but whether they take the final step or not, it's there and that's probably what the women who have taken the show and run with it have felt. It's almost not necessary to see it acted out, because it's there in full bloom. Playing that heat within the parameters of what we have to do it an interesting exercise."

A very real concern, naturally, is that what seems fresh and innovative now could turn into cliché as the series continues. This thought has not escaped the actor's attention.

"I'm fearful of that, sure," he said. "I've been very concerned about the premise of the show, and it's not as if it's falling on deaf ears. Ron Koslow is supervising every single script and every word that goes into every script, and he also knows that this can easily become *The Incredible Hulk* if we're not careful. Using the formula of her getting into trouble, his saving her during the last ten minutes, and the two of them walking off into the sunset is the last thing in the world we want to put in any episode. We're trying to figure out how not to do that; how to make each one almost like a feature film, and I think we've been pretty successful. I think there are times when we've gotten a little bit formula, but I think it's justified — that it follows what has come before in a very organic way.

"In the beginning, we were finding our way, and I'll admit there was a bit of formula, but even in the most formula of our scripts, there have always been elements of incredible beauty and abstractness that most other shows don't ever address. Our worst is something that I still think is better than a lot of what you see on TV, and it's the kind of show I've always dreamed of. I really got lucky to find one that is a television series which happens to feel like a movie every week."

WHATEVER LINDA HAMILTON'S FEELINGS ABOUT TELEVISION, THERE WAS NO DENYING GENUINE CHEMISTRY BETWEEN HER AND RON PERLMAN. (PHOTO: CBS).

EPISODE GUIDE

The following episode guide for all three seasons of *Beauty and the Beast* is presented primarily through the eyes of writer/producers George R.R. Martin, Howard Gordon, Alex Gansa, David Peckinpah, Shelly Moore, Linda Campanelli and P.K. Simonds, Jr. and directors Victor Lobl, Gus Trikonis, Alan Cooke, and Richard Franklin.

SEASON ONE

Episode 1.1
The Pilot
"Once Upon A Time in the City of New York"
Original Airdate: September 25, 1987
Written by Ron Koslow
Directed by Richard Franklin
Regular Cast: Linda Hamilton (Catherine Chandler), Ron Perlman (Vincent), Roy Dotrice (Father), Jay Acovone (Joe Maxwell)
Guest Starring: Bill Marcus (D.A. Moreno), Tony Mockus, Jr. (Lt. Herman), Jason Allen (Kipper), John Petlock (Surgeon), Don Stark (Stocky Guy), John McMartin (Charles Chandler), Ron O'Neal (Isaac Stubbs), Ray Wise (Tom)

As noted earlier, *Beauty and the Beast* began with the Koslow-written pilot "Once Upon a Time... in the City of New York," which introduced the characters and set up the premise of the series. The pilot was directed by Richard Franklin, whose films had most definitely established him as a filmmaker in the Alfred Hitchcock vein.

What follows is an interview with Franklin (who passed away in 2007), which stands as the most in depth discussion he's had in print on the making of the pilot.

How did your involvement with Beauty and the Beast *come about?*

I got a call from my agent and he said, "There's a script here for a pilot that might interest you." It was by Ron Koslow, and I knew Ron's work from

Into the Night. Indeed, I had read a straighter draft of the script than the one John Landis landed up filming, which I appeared in. I thought, "Well, gee, this should be interesting," because Ron's a good writer. So I read it and liked it very much. I have been a fan of the Cocteau film for quite some time, needless to say. I wasn't quite sure what we were going to do or how that was going to work in a modern context, but I thought, why not? I came over and did it. It's not a terribly exciting story (laughs), but that's how it came about. It's the way most things happen, other than a project which you initiate yourself, like *Link* [a thriller about intellectually enhanced apes] which took six years to get made. The nice thing about television is that it happens quickly. It's not a situation where in six months, *if* the right elements come together we might make this. It's kind of like, "Can you come to New York on Thursday?" and that's literally what I did. I left the Australian summer and my next memory was climbing along some girders on the Manhattan Bridge, which was a location we were going to film, but ended up not doing so. Anyway, it was quite peculiar, but I've always wanted to film in New York so this gave me the opportunity.

What is it about New York that you find so attractive?

It's just a city that I find attractive. Do I have to tell a New Yorker? I've been getting to New York as often as I can on my sort of yo-yo life over the Pacific over the last fifteen years. I've been buying round trip tickets to New York as often as I could; trying to spend a week there while a script was being read or I wanted to get someone interested in a project. I just find it an exciting place and I wanted to film there.

You have no aversion going from films to television?

The first thing, I suppose, you have to understand is that most Australian directors, because our industry has been small or nonexistent prior to the early seventies, all crossed over and still do. Peter Weir still does commercials on occasion as I do.

You do?

Oh sure. Not here, but in Australia. I'm not saying that I wouldn't do them here, but I haven't. Funnily enough, people don't really make that crossover here. Although point two is the fact that recently it would appear, and I can't corroborate this except to say there's been articles about it in *American Film* and other places, noting that a number of feature directors have done, specifically, television pilots. From my point of view, it provided some sort of income regulation, because of residuals and additional payments if the show gets picked up and it goes for a second season and so on. It's attractive in that way. The other thing that's particularly attractive is that it's quick. You can spend 12 or 18 months or longer on a feature and then, as in the case of *Link*, have the frustration of seeing it disappear in a matter of days. It just doesn't warrant that amount of time. Admittedly in theory, a television show airs only once. I know that's not really true, but in theory you're just going for one hour as opposed to even one week. That somehow seemed more worthwhile to me, because it has all the creative rewards, and it's wonderfully quick. *Link* had been such a slow experience on so many levels, and I'm a director who likes to work fast, on the set in particular. I thought it would be a challenge to do television. I started in television, of course, directing a couple of year's worth of the show in Australia during the early 70s before I did my first feature.

It was a cop show wasn't it?

Yes, more or less. There are many attractions to *Beauty and the Beast*: New York, television, money, and probably most of all, the actual material, which I found interesting because like most things that attract me, it was in a grey area where one's first reaction might be to say, "Boy, this really might not work," which is the reaction when you look at *Beauty and the Beast* as a television show. One's immediate response is to say, "That sounds iffy." Well, that's always what attracts me creatively: Projects that are on a tightrope between being magical and being mundane, and I try to keep it as much a magical situation that I can.

It's really quite wonderful, and I hope the series can live up to what you did in the pilot.

I have no way of answering. The difficulty I think they're going to have is that *Beauty and the Beast* is a fantasy that sustains through to a transformation; that is, the beast turns into a prince. The longer the show goes on, the longer they're holding back on that transformation. I'm not saying that there are any plans to ever have him transforming into a prince, but there is a big payoff in the original film and story, which is that he turns into a prince so that everything turns out happily. The difficulty in doing the show week after week is that he can't turn into a prince at the end, so the stories are always kind of open-ended and the relationship between Beauty and the Beast is not moving towards a conclusion in the same way that it does in the original.

But the interesting thing about the pilot, I discovered, as opposed to a movie, is you're trying to lay out things open-ended because you're trying to whet the appetite of the audience for things to come, so it's an interesting form because you keep coming up with conflicts and complexities which you then don't resolve, which is fun in a pilot, but it may be hard to sustain.

What do you think it's got going for it that might make it a success?

I think its unique tonality, that it is a fantasy and quite a romantic one. It's old-fashioned. I don't mean 50s or 60s. What I mean is Victorian. It's a fantasy of literature of a hundred years ago. So it has a type of romanticism that I think is unique. I don't know where else on television I see such things. I think the most interesting thing in it is the relationship between Beauty and the Beast. And to me what's also interesting is this other world, this fantasy underworld if you like, which as opposed to the alligators of the New York sewer system image, is an image of an almost medieval kingdom under the streets of New York, just highly fanciful but I think extremely interesting and appealing. To me, that will sustain much interest, and the fact that the underworld is juxtaposed with New York. It's like the antithesis of New York, and I think that's interesting. Without in any way belittling Linda Hamilton's lead role — because I think she plays a very interesting character and is a wonderful actress — I think Ron Perlman is astonishing in Rick Baker's makeup; it is one of the most charismatic things that I've ever seen. I don't know how else to describe him. He's one of the most appealing people imaginable. It was very funny, actually, because I got so used to seeing him in his makeup that on occasion he would arrive or leave the set without the makeup, I would kind of shrink back in the way that people would to the beast, because I got so used to seeing him as the beast and he looks so splendid, still vulnerable as the beast. Anyway, that's kind of a list of about five things that I think are appealing about the show. You can sort them out under headings if you like (laughs). I kind of went from one thing to another. I started with tonality and landed up with makeup.

The next question was to be what is the appeal to you but I think you just answered that.

As I said, the appeal is what usually appeals to me. Something on that dangerous sort of tightrope between being magical and mundane. My favorite things are things that when you think about them after you've seen them, and they've worked wonderfully, you think back and say, "My God, that really could have been nothing." What was magical could have been nothing.

Your trademark of suspense still came through in the show. I even felt suspense when Linda Hamilton slowly began removing the bandages from her head.

That sort of came with the script. I won't say that I was consciously working to build suspense. It's something that I do without a great deal of effort. I had some fun with the scene where she was abducted in the beginning, although that was more of an action scene, where the van drives across the screen from right to left, and when it's gone she's gone. That's the equivalent of someone saying, "One minute I was walking down the street, and the next minute I was hit over the head." You don't see the person coming who hits you. That's what I tried to go for there, and then I would love to have done that scene for cinema. We had this metallic rubber floor put in the van so that I could really make it look like these guys were roughhousing her around. In truth, the van is actually like a gym mat. That was probably a subtlety that goes by pretty quickly on a television screen. That scene was fun. The final set piece, in the dark house, was a contrivance to build a bit of suspense. I tried to make more of her coming up the stairs with the sound of the television in the distance, although in television you have to move along so much quicker. Suspense, by its nature, is moments of waiting for things to happen, but you tend to play suspense a little less on television and go for action. But conversely, in cinema we probably would have had difficulty showing in cuts the beast getting all the way across town to save her, whereas because of the television or commercial-like nature of television, we could make that conceit and get him across town in the time it took her to get down a flight of stairs (laughs), if you know what I mean.

I think what interested me most, other than what attracted me, was the challenge. I had to do several dialogue scenes, eight from memory, in which we did not see the beast as was the case with the shark in the first *Jaws*, because that was something we were holding back on, in which we could not see the girl's face because her face was "damaged." Well, I looked at that old *Twilight Zone* with Donna Douglas, "Eye of the Beholder," and I looked how it was done in that. It was done quite simply, just with camera moves and so on, and I did it with slightly more complicated camera moves, but that was slightly unusual for television, to shoot, in some cases, four or five page dialogue scenes in one shot. On television that's not often done. Unlike a movie, where you don't have to reach a finite running time, a one hour television show has to hit the running time within a second. It has to be 57 minutes, 27 seconds. There has to be an exact length that relates to commercial time and so on. So the more scenes you shoot in one shot, the less flexibility you've got if you mistimed the length of the scene. That approach was, I think, very unusual for television. It was dictated not by the desire to do clever things with the camera (for example, there's a 360 in one scene), but because I couldn't show either the face of the beauty or the face of the beast.

From memory there were eight scenes and from each scene I worked out a little scenario. I showed just a little more of the beast. One moment we saw just the cloak, then we'd see what color his hair was, eventually we see his hand, which I think was the first ad break, and then I was quite pleased the moment when she touches his hand and he recoils. I thought that moment worked out really well. The moment at which the Beast first appears, I really took directly from the Lon Chaney *Phantom of the Opera*. I had every intention of doing all sorts of fancy cuts and opticals with a shot of her looking at her own face in the mirror, and then suddenly he appears in the mirror and she turns around. I had quite an elaborate scenario worked out, but then I looked at *Phantom of the Opera* and realized that for whatever reason, that moment is one of the greatest reveals of all time and it's really just done in a cut. I didn't even do a cut. From memory I just had Ron stand behind Linda and at the moment she pulls the mirror down and we see her face for the first time without the bandages, I had him step up from behind her. He doesn't even come through the door. He sort of seems to come from her body. Intellectually that might sound interesting, but it was immensely simple and was based on the idea that we would be looking at the scars on her face in the way that one can't resist looking at car accidents and such things. As much as one doesn't want to. And then suddenly he would be there, and to me Rick Baker's makeup was so incredible that I didn't want to gild the lily.

Having seen the makeup, I decided that I wasn't going to turn this into a big, fancy cutting sequence. I would just let him step forward into the light and let the makeup do its job. So quite a bit of thought went into that and I could have been a lot more elaborate. It could have been played as much more of a shock moment, but it seemed to me that it wasn't entirely valid for the beast to be shocking.

An interesting scene is when the guys are approaching her, she screams and Vincent's head pops up, and it's intercut with him getting to her in time.

I think he turns his head, but anyway, that was kind of a good moment. As I say, that whole scene is a real conceit, because he couldn't possibly get across town in that time. He couldn't get on the train, let alone get to her. That sort of takes the conceit of the protracted television format, contracted rather, as per commercials, and use it to our advantage. As I say, in cinema we would have had to have her trapped in the house a lot longer, to justify his getting that distance. But in the shorter format of television, it was possible to bring him there almost in a montage. Yeah, that was kind of fun. I liked it too, and it had a sort of strange heroic quality, like a cavalry was coming to the rescue.

He takes care of the guys, then he notices Linda Hamilton staring at him. In that moment, his eyes soften and the roaring stops. Beautiful moment.

I would have liked to have played with that moment more, but there's the feeling in television that you have to get to your climax and get out quickly. He knows that she perceives him as an animal at that moment, and he feels remorse and guilt. I would love to have played more with that, but it's not the nature of television. I thought it was an important moment when she sees his animal side.

He is naked in front of her for the first time, so to speak.

And then we hear the sirens coming and she almost has to save *him*. If one played more with that moment, the idea would be that he would feel such guilt that he would surrender himself to the police because he feels like he's behaved as an animal. But she saves him instead.

Was the cast in place before you got there?

No. Ron Perlman had been selected, and I couldn't have been more delighted, but Linda came in literally at the eleventh hour. I was astonished, actually, that someone of her caliber would do this. Because they effectively sign on for about five years when they do a series. Having seen her in *The Terminator*, I was just knocked out at having someone of that caliber playing the girl. I guess she had her personal reasons for wanting to go back into television at this moment, and I think we were all lucky.

Roy Dotrice, who plays Ron Perlman's father, was someone that I was delighted to have an opportunity to work with. He's just one of the most amazing character actors...well, actors, to be honest. Character actors sound like they always play the same character. In fact, he always plays completely different characters. I don't say that most people would instantly realize that he was the father in *Amadeus*, for example. He has the most astonishing range of an actor. He's played Lincoln on Broadway and lots and lots of Shakespeare in England, and it was a thrill to work with someone that good. I remember when we did the scene in which he tells Vincent that he has to forget the girl, I rolled the cameras... it was very late at night, and we'd been waiting around all day to do the scene. It was like the last day of shooting in LA, and we had to finish this. From memory, Roy had been waiting for many hours and when we finished he asked me if I wanted to see it another way. I thought it was perfect the way it was and couldn't be improved and he said, "Let me show you another way." He did it a second time, did it just as well, but in an entirely different way. I can't remember which one we ended up using, but they were both equally good. A guy that good really doesn't need direction, and to do that after that many hours of waiting around, I was just blown away. But take a look at his credits, and you'll see that he's an amazing actor.

Would you say you brought anything to the pilot that would help define what the series would be?

I don't know, because I don't know which way the series has gone. That would be a better question to ask Ron Koslow. All I can say is that I think I set the tone of the piece. That's probably the thing I think about most. Once I know what the tone is, that is to what degree it's realistic, what degree it's fantasy, to what degree we're having fun with it, to what degree we're making fun of it, to what degree we're taking it seriously, to what degree it's romantic...I mean, all of those shadings are what concerns me in the first instance, and given that I am attracted to material that is hard to pull off, hard to make convincing, getting the tone right is immensely important to me. If we'd gone a bit too realistic or a bit too fairy tale, the whole thing could have collapsed. I think in that area I probably have dictated the direction they have to go. There's no question also that the first director who works with the actors on their characters, tends to define the way that the characters go. At least I imagine so. The other directors are probably cursing me now, because the actors have such a clear idea of what they want to do, and it comes from the evolution of the characters which I was fortunate enough to be there for and a party to.

I would say in those two areas, in tone and character, the one person who I think should be mentioned — apart from Rick Baker, who is a genius and deserves his reputation and who has a magnificent creation in Vincent — is Roy Wagner, the director of photography. He had just come off *Nightmare on Elm Street 3*. Roy had just shot that, and I had been wanting to work with him for years. He had shot some film with a colleague of mine from film school, and I had admired his style for a long time. The look of that show has so much to do with the lighting. I was able to stage things in a particular way because he's one of the first cameramen I've ever worked with to who if I ever said, "Now, it will be black over there..." That is, if I stand the Beast in that corner, he will be in the darkness, and with Roy I was always assured that that was the case. Cameramen are often tempted to put lights on for the sake of lighting, because they figure that's what they're doing. It's like asking a painter to leave a piece of the canvas blank if you ask them to leave part of the set dark. A lesser cameraman would have put the lights on, and I would have had to do it with the cutting. Whereas because of the way he lit those sets, particularly the underground, I was able to stage scenes in a much more interesting way, because I could rely on him to keep the beast in shadow. Very often there's not much logic to that. Where, for example, you want there to be light on the girl's face, but not light on the beast's face. It is not logical from the point of view of the physics of lighting, but it is emotionally apt that the Beast be a dark figure and the girl be a light figure. Well, more than emotionally. Obviously it's symbolism. A lot of cameramen would be emphatic and say that I can't stand them next to each other and have one of them in light and the other in darkness. But Roy, who is a great cameraman, was not only willing to do that, but able to do that. I'm not sure how many modern cameramen can light in that style.

That underground was incredible.

He's really a great cameraman, and when you ask me to what extent I dictated where the show went, I believe he had every bit as much to do with that. In fact, the first four or five episodes of the show were also shot by him. They asked him to stay on just to keep that look going into the series itself. He has not done episodic TV before, so it was a major step for him to turn down features and do more episodes. But he did, because he cared enough about the show.

It's great when you have that much enthusiasm from the crew.

Philosophically I'm very much with Andy Warhol. I believe that what we consider to be artistically important and what is really of cultural significance are entirely different things. I'm talking about the Campbell's Soup can painting. What we consider to be lofty and what really is meaningful, are two quite different things. I'm not saying that I'm necessarily a pop artist, but I'm saying it's possible to say something is meaningful in a television commercial, given the time restrictions and the fact you're trying to sell something , as it is a feature film, from my point of view. There's no difference. I think one should not take an elitist approach to art and culture. That's my qualification. But unquestionable is that for a feature cameraman to then do episodic television, it's a dubious career move, and Roy did that because he cared enough about the show. In fact, he shot the pilot because just as I wanted to work with him, he wanted to work with me. I think anyone looking at that show will see a style of lighting that just has not ever been seen on television, other than old movies that are shown on television. Under the ground, because of the period setting, it was quite apt to go for a style of sort of a gothic expressionist lighting, which would not have been appropriate for above the ground modern New York. We went for a different look in both places.

In your estimation, what can an audience expect from Beauty and the Beast?

That's an awfully hard question. I think they can expect to be surprised (laughs). I'm not saying that that's what I set out to do, but I was surprised when I read the script, you were surprised when you saw the pilot...everyone seems to react that way. I don't know why, because I don't know too many people who don't like the Jean Cocteau film. I think they thought that commercial television would not mesh with such fare, if you know what I mean. While I don't think we've achieved what Cocteau did, it was interesting...I was reading his diary while we were shooting. He wrote a diary of the making of *Beauty and the Beast*, and one thing that he said early on is that "fantasy is such a brittle thing," that he took the view that what he should do was approach the thing not as if he was making a magical jewel box, but as if he was making a table. Something functional and simple, and straight-forward and solid. That's the way I approached this, and I think even I was surprised how those magical moments in a story that's lasted more than a hundred years, kind of surfaced and were appealing. I think the other subplot, the sort of crime story that might superficially be significant, tends to become secondary to what was the secondary element...in fact, the element that I didn't even go for while I was directing, which is the element of fantasy, of romance as in *Wuthering Heights*; the romance of the Victorian romantic novelists. Those secondary elements surfaced on their own and surprised even me. I hoped that that's what would happen, and it did, and I have Cocteau to thank for that. I think if we'd worked at the fantasy, we might have lost it. It could have vanished. I think the audience could expect to be surprised.

What's more, and this goes back to your first question of how the thing came about, I must say that I'm a little tired of the modern cinema, particularly where fantasy cinema, particularly where the fantasy-horror genre, is concerned, and it's a genre I've concerned myself with. I'm tired of having to reduce all stories to the lowest common denominator of what will appeal to twelve year olds. And I'm afraid that that's what one is continually forced to do when one works in this genre. I'm not saying that when you make *Plenty* or *Out of Africa* that you're not making a film for adults, but the minute you make fantasy for the modern cinema, you're thinking what will scare twelve year olds, what will be interesting and exciting for twelve year olds. I have an eleven year old daughter, so I'm not putting them down, but what I'm saying is that some stories, and I think *Beauty and the Beast* is one of them, do not necessarily come down easily to the level of a 12 year old. It was extremely refreshing, and a real paradox if you think about it, to be able to make this for adults. What I mean by that is look at the demographics. The marketing experts tell you that when you're making cinema, particularly for this genre, that you're aiming at the young teenagers and up to 20 at the absolute outside. You look at the demographics of the television audience, and you're mostly aiming at families and or married people with kids, in their late 20s through their 50s and 60s, and it is possible, as paradoxical as it sounds, to actually be a little more adult in your sensibilities. And that, to me, was refreshing. I know that sounds paradoxical and quite unlike what one does in commercial television, but I have to tell you that in recent films that I've made there has been so much pressure to always think of the 12 year olds.

The thing about aiming for 12 year olds. Do you think that's more based on fact or the studios' opinion?

Without opening a can of worms here, I think that there is a tendency among distributors in particular to underestimate their audiences. I could go further than that. Maybe I will. I think sometimes there's a tendency among distributors to hold their audience in contempt. I suppose you can't blame them when you see the way some people behave in movie theatres, but I think it leads to a particularly low lowest common denominator being dictated to filmmakers by distributors. The idea is, "Listen, what they want is of the standard of the stuff we sell at the concession stand. They want popcorn movies. They don't want filet steak." And it's often hard to convince them that you can give them filet steak often at the same price. They almost don't want to give them filet steak. I think it comes from underestimating the public, which I know is what P.T, Barnum said makes you rich. I think it goes one worse than that. Maybe I just came off a bad experience with Cannon on *Link*, but I think distributors en masse tend to hold their audience in contempt, and I don't agree with that. I would rather overestimate an audience's intelligence, which is basically what I did with *Psycho II*. I could not have pitched that at much more of an intellectual level than I did, to be honest, and we didn't lose money by overestimating the American public.

The wonderful thing to me was watching that movie with a midnight audience in Time Square. You can imagine what kind of audience that was, but the astonishing thing was they were not experts on *Psycho* in the way that you and I are, yet I swear to you every subtlety in that movie communicated to that audience. I'm not saying that they could come out afterwards and discuss the light motifs, in the way that we could, but it did not go over their heads. In other words, they conveyed, or communicated, at an emotional level every nuance of that picture. I am not of the P.T. Barnum School. I would rather go in the other direction. I don't know if you can actually, because on that I agree with Frank Capra, even if individually the audience doesn't have the I.Q. that one might wish them to have, en masse there's this peculiar thing, and a group of people together seem to respond according to the highest intellectual level among them. The minute that one person picks up on something, it goes through the audience like a wave, and so a group of people has a higher I.Q. than any individual. That's not my idea, it's Frank Capra's, and I think it's absolutely true. Sure there are certain instances where people respond like a mob, but when they're watching movies, they tend to be extremely sophisticated and extremely intelligent. I don't like this notion that we've to bring it down to the level of the 12 year olds. It would be wonderful to say that a 12 year old has such an incredibly innate sense of storytelling that we should bring it up to a 12 year old level, but the word down is always used. The minute they say, "We're trying to appeal to the 12 year old," they say, "Let's bring it down to their level." That I don't like. Fortunately you don't have to do that on television. So that's yet another reason why I liked to do *Beauty and the Beast*.

Episode 1.2
"Terrible Savior"
Original Airdate: October 2, 1987
Written by George R.R. Martin
Directed by Alan Cooke
Guest Starring: Dorian Harewood (Jason Walker), Tracee Lyles (Mrs. Dalby), Delroy Lindo (Isaac Stubbs)

When a vigilante strikes back against subway crime using claws and leaving victims looking as though they've been mauled by a lion, Catherine fears that she may be viewing the handiwork of Vincent.

"The episode was originally called 'Terrible Angel,' until the legal department got nervous, thinking the Guardian Angels might sue us for using 'Angel.' It's not one of my favorite episodes," notes its author, George R.R. Martin. "Some of it was my fault. I think I was a little too ambitious. Despite my experience in *Twilight Zone*, I was still relatively new at writing for television. When you write books, you have an unlimited special effects budget. The initial draft had a climactic battle on top of a moving subway car, as Vincent and Jase hurtle from car to car and fought with each other. This would be great for a $20 million movie, but it was not doable on our budget. In fact, the whole script posed production problems for them. There were no real subways that we could shoot out in Los Angeles, as we soon discovered. We were fortunate enough to find a standing subway car for an exterior, and an interior car that we borrowed. We had to fairly curtail some of the subway material, which was strange for an episode about a subway vigilante.

"The very first shot is when you see the shape rushing down the car to kill the first two people," he adds. "I think most people recognized it was not Vincent, which was not the intent. In the teleplay, I asked for a strobe effect, with the light in the car going out, so the only light would be coming in through the windows as the car shoots through a lit station. Most of that scene should have been played in darkness or near darkness, and the idea was to create the possibility that it *was* Vincent. You have to remember that at the time neither the writers nor the audience nor Catherine knew Vincent very well. So the dilemma, Catherine's fear of Vincent's ability to kill, I think was still something that could be played. That was really the thematic point of the script."

"CATHERINE'S FEAR OF VINCENT'S ABILITY TO KILL, I THINK WAS STILL SOMETHING THAT COULD BE PLAYED," SAYS GEORGE R.R. MARTIN OF "TERRIBLE SAVIOR".

Says Howard Gordon, "Catherine had just met Vincent, and while she had an undeniable connection to him, there was a fear of him as well. 'Terrible Savior' was born out of an exploration of that fear. This man, who she'd seen rip apart three men in the pilot...how dangerous was he? What other circumstance would bring out that kind of rage? When she actually suspects he might be the killer, which is just a momentary thing, it breaks Vincent's heart. He basically leaves it to her to decide. He doesn't deny her that. Even George would admit that there was a slightly cartoony element to it. But, it moves and there was some good action in it."

"Not my favorite episode," adds Alex Gansa, "and I don't think it was anyone's fault. Largely because the final confrontation between Vincent and Jase was just anti-climactic. It was also at the very beginning stages when we were trying to find out what stories would work. I thought there were some wonderful things in it, but I think the whole thing got muddled. What was interesting was the whole nature of vigilantism and what place it had. And how it related to Vincent as a character and the nature of his ripping people to shreds. Was there any ambiguity or grayness about what was going on? I just thought that got lost and muddled in the context of the story. Another problem is that we were always walking this line of not only how much does Catherine fear Vincent, but how much could she love him? What were the boundaries of the relationship? I think we always erred on the side of safety, unfortunately. I think that was a big problem of the second season as well."

The show's director, Alan Cooke, notes, "I thought the script was an interesting one that gave a very good possibility to the mythic parallel, because you had the two monsters, as it were. I thought it was a particularly successful link there. The Jason Walker character was most interesting to me, and formed a very nice reversal...mirror image...of the Beast. The Beast is fierce on the outside and very gentle within, while Jason was the other way around."

Martin feels that if "Terrible Savior" served any purpose, it helped create a little more of the underground "reality."

"It introduced the Whispering Gallery, which was the first kind of really magical chamber down there," he explains. "If you look at the pilot, which is all any of us had seen before, there are tunnels down there, subways, sewers and steam tunnels — essentially very realistic things. When I invented the Whispering Gallery, it was a deliberate attempt to make that underworld a little more mythic and a little more extraordinary. I wasn't sure it would be accepted at first. I was concerned that people at the network would not want these wondrous semi-magical chambers under New York, but fortunately everybody greeted the notion with great enthusiasm. Subsequently, I added some chambers myself, Ron Koslow added the waterfall chamber, I came up with the chamber of winds, Howard and Alex came up with the crystal cavern. There was a process of that world growing. It was very organic in a sense; we were all sort of feeding off of each other once we gathered together for our story session. It was not a case where we sat down one day and said, 'Let's plan this world' and got out this map-drawing thing.

"We had a few odd lapses in continuity if you're a real stickler. In those scenes in the Whispering Gallery, Father walks in and his first line is, 'The children have told me of this place,' like he's never been there before. And Vincent sort of explains to him how it works. Clearly, the dialogue as established in the script is that Vincent played here in his youth, but it was sort of a secret place and Father never came there. Of course as the series developed, people started passing through that area every time they went to the bathroom. Clearly, it became — geographically — one of the closest of the magical chambers to whatever underground areas our people lived near. There are a lot of scenes that take place there, which makes the dialogue in that first episode rather unsmooth. It's just the way things work."

Episode 1.3
"Siege"
Original Airdate: October 9, 1987
Written by David E. Peckinpah
Directed by Paul Lynch
Guest Starring: Edward Albert, Jr. (Elliot Burch), Herta Ware (Sylvia), Stuart Charno (Bennie)

Catherine starts to fall in love with Elliot Burch in "Siege," in which the real estate magnate, unbeknownst to her, is having a gang of punks try to drive a group of elderly people out of a building whose property he wants to purchase. He is not aware of the fact that said punks are terrorizing the tenants to the extent that they are, and it is up to Catherine and Vincent to set things right. Naturally by episode's end she realizes that Vincent is her true love.

"I thought 'Siege' represented the proper balance between Catherine's life and Vincent's life," says David Peckinpah. "It also introduced us to Elliot Burch, and I think Edward Albert, Jr. did a fabulous job and became a very important player."

Comments Gansa, "Siege' was one of my favorite episodes, mostly because the Vincent and Catherine stuff was just so fantastic. The rest of the material which had very little bearing on the relationship was just the excuse with which to bring them into contact. All the shows had a conventional TV aspect, which is what we called the 'shoe leather,' and that was hopefully leading to some kind of moment between Vincent and Catherine. In 'Siege,' it was the old people. It made the network more comfortable

THE LATE EDWARD ALBERT, JR. PORTRAYED REAL ESTATE MAGNATE
ELLIOT BURCH, A POTENTIAL LOVE INTEREST FOR CATHERINE.

with what we were doing. They could see familiar aspects that they could understand."

Gordon notes that "Siege" was "a very successful episode. It introduced Elliot Burch and what that show did, thematically, was deal with the impossibility of their relationship and the inevitability that she would eventually have to pursue a life with someone else. I think that show did it really, really well. But how many times can Catherine and Vincent be jealous, and how many men can Catherine go out with before it reduces the entire relationship? One of the things we tried to do from the very beginning was counterpoint the world Above, and that world was the glitzy world of Manhattan, the Ivory Tower. Elliot Burch also came out nicely in the episode."

Episode 1.4
"No Way Down"
Original Airdate: October 16, 1987
Written by James Crocker
Directed by Thomas J. Wright
Guest Starring: Mayim Bialik (Ellie), Paul T. Murray (Tony), Fran Montano (Grimes), Bernie Pock (Sco), Merritt Butrick (Shake), Jeffrey Combs (Python), Delroy Lindo (Isaac Stubbs)

In "No Way Down," Vincent is blinded in an explosion, and captured by a group of gang members who proceed to torture him. Escaping, but still unable to see, Vincent must make his way back to the tunnels.

"Program standards didn't want us to make the episode, because they thought it was too violent," explains David Peckinpah. "They thought it would scare children and that it was putting Vincent in jeopardy, in a situation that was too intense. Actually, the look of it was great, resembling a Walter Hill movie. It was also the highest rated episode of the first season. In a strange way, I think it was 'No Way Down' which prompted them to go with more violent stories, because of the ratings. When they reran it, the show did a big rating as well."

Howard Gordon says, "That was a remarkably popular episode and it also ran $400,000 over budget. At the time, we didn't know if we were going to be on the air, and the way the show was financed, that was a terrible burden. I think it came out really well. Again, we were trying to find interesting stories to tell. This was probably the first parable. Straight up action with a lot of tension, dealing with this kind of mythical gang."

"An episode that almost killed us," laughs George R.R. Martin. "It went enormously over budget. Originally, the fourth act climax was set in a cemetery, and we couldn't find a cemetery that would let us shoot at night, and shoot guns off and set off explosions. Understandably, some cemeteries are fussy about that kind of thing. We found cemeteries that would let us shoot during the day, cemeteries that would let us do special effects, but none that would fit all of those criteria. Tom Wright, the director, had filmed *Max Headroom* in a place down in Long Beach which was an old, abandoned men's club. A tremendously atmospheric old building. The script was rewritten to fit the athletic club, and because of all the night shooting (which is very expensive) it was running over budget anyway. It was only the fourth episode and the crew was quite new and we weren't used to doing things. When we actually got down there, someone started the rumor that the whole place was filled with asbestos, and there was a crew walkout and we lost an entire day's shooting. That is enormously expensive — a couple of hundred thousand dollars down the tubes, and various grievances were filed against us. Well, in point of fact, later on investigations showed that there was no asbestos in the building. It was a complete fabrication.

"We very rapidly shifted to a third location the following day, and we wound up in an atmospheric closed-up bank building. The whole thing produced an episode that was like $400,000 over budget, the most any episode ever went over. Nonetheless, it's a show that I think turned out very well. Tom Wright did a terrific job directing it and we had some wonderful guest stars."

"I hate that episode," counters Alex Gansa. "I know everybody loves it and thought it was fantastic. I was just appalled at the violence in that episode. I just didn't buy that group as a gang. It seemed to be very farcical. Put it this way, at the time we were doing it, I couldn't believe that this is what the show was going to be about. I had envisioned a completely other vision for the course of the show, and it staggered me to see this. I saw the show going a much softer route, much less violent and much more romantic."

Episode 1.5
"Masques"
Original Airdate: October 30, 1987
Written by George R.R. Martin
Directed by Alan Cooke
Guest Starring: Cory Danziger (Kipper), Kimberly McCullough (Abbey), Caitlin O'Heaney (Briget O'Donnell), John McMartin (Charles Chandler), Eric Pierpoint (Donald), Aubrey Morris (Sean)

"Masques" was *Beauty and the Beast's* Halloween show, representing the one day a year that Vincent can walk the Earth among men. He and Catherine get mixed up with an Irish poet and the terrorists out to kill her.

"When I came on the show," explains the episode's writer, George R.R. Martin, "I came in with two story ideas. One of them was 'Masques' and the other was 'Terrible Angel,' which had jeopardy, a subway vigilante and all that. I wanted 'Masques' to be very different, and I wanted it to be a very romantic, kind of magic episode with mystery and the pageantry of Halloween night. I didn't necessarily want a strong jeopardy element in it. I wanted to make it almost picturesque, with Catherine and Vincent out on Halloween night and encountering the strange sights of New York City, seeing parts of the city they'd never seen before — little moments of romance and little moments of humor, mystery and action. But the network was still coming down very heavily at that end and they said, 'No, you have to have jeopardy if you want to do this. You have to have guys with guns.' I was initially upset about this and we had some arguments about it. I said, 'Wait a minute, you got me out here to write this under the premise that this was going to be adult drama, not formula action/adventure, and suddenly we have the formula. I don't like it much.' I kicked and screamed, but ultimately the network was very insistent on that, and of course that came down through the studio, Ron and so forth. So, I went back and had to come up with an action subplot, and that was the Irish question."

As originally conceived, this would have been the episode that introduced former tunnel world dweller Devin, more or less Vincent's "brother."

"When I did come up with the Irish plot that was going to be the episode where I introduced Devin," Martin explains. "I had that notion of a Devin character in mind right from the beginning. The early storyline had the party being held for this world famous journalist, and Father having a strange, cryptic conversation about when Vincent wants to go. You realize there's a past with this person, but you don't quite know what it is. Then, Vincent goes up and confronts Devin, and there was a scene where you don't know if they're going to attack each other or not. It's never made clear what the relationship between them is. But they end by embracing each other. Then, Devin goes down to confront Father and his own past, while Vincent stays Above with Catherine. It was kind of a 'Prince and the Pauper' kind of story. At that stage, the network was approving all of our stories at least in rough form. That didn't last long. It ended, I'd say, about a third of the way through the first season. So, Ron Koslow and, I guess, [producers] Tony [Thomas] or Paul [DeWitt], went over to meet with Kim LeMasters, and came back. They took my story and everybody else's. Then, they came back and said that LeMasters wasn't too keen on the brother idea, but he liked the idea of a women poet. So I figured out a way to put in a women poet, and I never forgot about Devin. He arrived later in the season when we were a lot freer and the stories didn't need approval. I was able to do 'Promise of Someday,' which was a real character piece and very little in the way of action. I think all told I'm pretty happy with the way it turned out, although I wasn't happy at the time."

Adds director Alan Cooke, "'Masques' was an episode they were most anxious about. They asked me to do it because they felt I had an intuitive sense of what the Beast was. That was one of the trickiest ones, because it involved his appearing in public, almost unmasked, as it were. The nice concept is that on Halloween night he can walk around and everyone would think it was a cute make-up. At the same time, the producers were very concerned, because in a sense it tested the theory to the outermost. They were always afraid that it would look like a man wearing a cat mask. So suddenly, here he was being able to walk around because he looked like a man wearing a cat mask. It sort of ripped the seams off the entire concept, and reminded us that it was just an actor. They always wanted to keep around Vincent the aura of mystery that he was not a man who dressed up; that he was not really a human at all. That was a nice challenge."

"I wish we could have found more episodes to do like that one," says Alex Gansa. "Any time Vincent could interface in a logical way with the world Above, it was fantastic. Halloween was just the perfect setting, and I'm really sorry we didn't get to do another Halloween episode. It was just wonderful to see Vincent out among the living, as opposed to buried underneath the Earth. The whole Irish thing was interesting, but I liked some of the *Midsummer Night's Dream* quality it had. Again, I could have done without the shoe-leather, the crazy gun-toting terrorist. That stuff was silly. Seeing Vincent and Catherine in that Woody Allen pose on the park bench at the ending was fantastic."

Howard Gordon enthuses, "I love that episode, Halloween being the only day of the year that Vincent can walk among men. George had an idea for another Halloween episode for the second season, a story worked out, but because of the [1988 Writer's] strike we couldn't air a show near Halloween, so we never did it."

Episode 1.6
"The Beast Within"
Original Airdate: November 6, 1987
Written by Andrew Laskos
Directed by Paul Lynch
Guest Starring: Bill Marcus (D.A. Moreno), Michael J. London (Shanks), Jack McGee (McQuade), Asher Brauner (Mitch Denton), John McLiam (Sam Denton)

In "The Beast Within," former tunnel denizen Mitch Denton, who had a falling out with Father years earlier, has turned to a life of crime in the world Above, threatening the life of innocent dock workers and, of course, Catherine. This does *not* sit well with Vincent.

"That storyline," explains Howard Gordon, "came about by the need to show that not everybody who came out of the tunnel world was a saint. Again, part of it was to show some of Vincent's past. Thematically, I think it worked pretty well."

George Martin doesn't concur. "I was never that fond of 'Beast Within'," he says, "but that's more a personal thing. I think it works pretty well, but I had originally devised the Devin character for 'Masques' and he had been removed from that episode because of network dictates. Then, 'Beast Within' came along with the Mitch Denton character, and another kind of quasi-brother that Vincent had known in his childhood. Of course, for that reason, it stole a certain amount of Devin's thunder when I finally got to use him in 'Promises of Someday.'"

Episode 1.7
"Nor Iron Bars a Cage"
Original Airdate: November 13, 1987
Written by Howard Gordon & Alex Gansa
Directed by Thomas J. Wright
Guest Starring: Michael Ensign (Edward Hughes), Christian Clemenson (Gould), Basil Hoffman (Trask), Darryl Hickman (Quint), Ellen Albertini Dow (Anna Lausch)

"Nor Iron Bars a Cage" had Vincent trapped Above ground again, only this time he's captured by a pair of scientists, one humane and the other with no scruples whatsoever.

"I thought there were some fantastic moments in that show, and I'm speaking completely biased because I wrote that one with Howard," laughs Alex Gansa. "Again, I thought it was the kind of episode we should have done more of. The violence was very contained. It was graphic when it happened, but it was not interspersed throughout the show. The issues at stake were Catherine and Vincent being separated. Catherine and Vincent shows were always our most successful episodes. We also had the issue that Catherine, who had decided to take a job in Rhode Island, having just told Vincent that she's leaving, and then having to search for him and realizing the depths of her love. It also alluded to Vincent's origins, which were fascinating. It was an episode that, to me, had all the ingredients there. Whether we executed it properly, who knows? It had all the stuff in it that was important."

Howard Gordon states that the episode came from an idea supplied by actor Ron Perlman. "Alex and I ran with it," he explains, "and came up with the show. Perlman's idea was that a scientist from the world Above captures him. That was an exploration of what Vincent's nature really is, and a poetic approach in that you look at a beast and at first you think he's a beast, but there's so much more to him. One of my favorite scenes is the one between him and the professor, and kind of echoes Shylock and *The Merchant of Venice* saying, 'If you cut me, I'll bleed.' All in all it was a good episode, and I think Perlman was nominated for an Emmy for that show."

Episode 1.8
"Song of Orpheus"
Original Airdate: November 20, 1987
Written by Howard Gordon & Alex Gansa
Directed by Peter Medak
Guest Starring: Stan Lachow (Parker), Clive Rosengren (Lou), Gary Berner (Conor), Diana Douglas (Margaret Chase), Paul Gleason (Henry Dutton), Robert Symonds (Alan Taft)

"Song of Orpheus" is an episode focusing on Father, exploring his past in the world Above as he returns to see his dying former wife.

"This was the first thing we wrote for the show, and was supposed to be the second episode until Roy Dotrice fell into the deep end of a pool and was completely immobile," relates Howard Gordon. "I'm very happy with the episode, but I believe it could have been better. An earlier draft Alex and I had written included a Council scene and at that point the network was arguing that there were too many people Below. We had some story where a young family had a child. In the episode Father gets caught by the police, but had been a period [in the script] where we explored the possibility of Vincent taking over as the leader of the world Below. We had some story where a young family had a child and they needed to have a dwelling built, and Vincent basically oversees this operation. We introduced it in a very uplifting way, counterpointing it with Father's absence, and also brought up the notion of Vincent assuming the mantle at one point.

"Also in an earlier draft, it was a much softer story. Father goes Above and learns that his former lover has married his old-ex partner from the McCarthy days, who it turns out, had basically framed him and turned him in to the Un-American Activities Committee to get the woman, to destroy his life....and it was a much more organic kind of story. The network felt it was too soft, that we would have two 70-year-old men and an old woman. They wanted something a little more hard edged. On two levels, that show was a disappointment, although in the end, I was happy with the way it came out."

Says Alex Gansa, "'Song of Orpheus' could have been a great episode. Basically, it was our own fear that made it not so great. I happen to think there are things about that episode which are fantastic — Father's past

ACCLAIMED ACTOR ROY DOTRICE WAS CAST AS FATHER, LEADER OF THE
TUNNEL COMMUNITY AND VINCENT'S PATERNAL FIGURE.

and his McCarthy hearing run-ins — and I think it explained a hell of a lot about what he was doing down there, it explained a lot of his philosophy, his hurt and his pain. In that way, I thought it was a breakthrough episode for us because it explained so much, but what happened was that it just got diluted by the charity worker who was keeping Father's ex-wife hostage with pills. That was a never anyone's intention on staff. That was a network note. They really wanted a black hat villain who Vincent could kill. That's what that character became. Howard and I fought so hard not to kill this guy at the end. If you remember what happened, he was trapped in an elevator. Vincent comes in through the roof and pulls Catherine out. As I recall, nobody died in that episode, which was always Howard's and my wish. We never wanted to kill anybody. We worked so hard that Vincent didn't have to rip anybody to shreds. We wanted to minimize the death and destruction. Although it was a bastardized episode, because we weren't able to do the triangle between Father, his ex-partner and the woman, I felt it was a good episode with a lot of wonderful material."

Episode 1.9
"Dark Spirit"
Original Airdate: November 27, 1987
Written by Robin Bernheim
Directed by Thomas J. Wright
Guest Starring: Beah Richards (Narcissa), David Sabin (Arthur), Gary Carlos Cervantes (Rafael Cruz), Cliff DeYoung (Alexander Ross), Diana Barton (Lindsay Gates)

Catherine investigates a voodoo murder, and finds herself a victim of its black magic, which turns her against Vincent.

"Dark disappointment," muses Howard Gordon. "It just didn't work. Part of it was that it wasn't one of our favorites. Voodoo is a tough thing to do right. What it did do was introduce Narcissa, an interesting character. When it's done right and interestingly, voodoo can be worth doing. I think it was just a missed opportunity."

"The worst episode we ever did," concurs Alex Gansa. "It was just an abortion from square one. I tend to block it out of my brain, because it was just terrible. The story wasn't there, it wasn't shot particularly well."

Episode 1.10
"A Children's Story"
Original Airdate: December 4, 1987
Written by Ron Koslow
Directed by Gabrielle Beaumont
Guest Starring: Nike Doukas (Margaret), Rachel Resnikoff (Deb), Richard Herd (Richard Barnes), Kamie Harper (Ellie), Richard Portnow (Naj), Joshua Rudoy (Eric)

A modern retelling of *Oliver Twist*, with children being stolen from orphanages and sold to a Fagin-like thief.

"We tried very hard to make this show different from everything else on the air," says George R.R. Martin, "but this episode was pretty standard television."

Alex Gansa observes, "An okay episode. I like the Dickensian quality about it. That episode was written very early on — it was shot after the pilot — and it was a learning process for everyone."

Says Howard Gordon, "Actually, it was the very first episode written and shot. It was also a disappointment. I don't think the emotional truth was there. I'm not sure what went wrong with it, except that maybe it was a little flat dramatically."

Episode 1.11
"An Impossible Silence"
Original Airdate: December 18, 1987
Written by Howard Gordon & Alex Gansa
Directed by Christopher Leitch
Guest Starring: Armin Shimerman (Pascal), Terrylene (Laura Williams), Michael Lewis (Costanza), Kathleen Heller (Sharon Lewis), Virginia Watson (Sgt. Walker), Chris Mulkey (Danny Yates)

Laura, a deaf girl from Below, witnesses a murder Above, and ultimately chooses to testify in "An Impossible Silence."

"I don't know what prompted the script crisis," relates Howard Gordan, "but Alex and I had to write it in four or five days, and it came out very well. It was very exciting because it introduced a character who we were all very attached to. I think it stretched the actors a little bit, and it presented the issue of the disabled."

Alex Gansa, who co-wrote the episode with Gordan, admits to liking it very much. "The actress who played Laura [Terrylene], was fantastic," he enthuses. "And the whole business of the deaf witness worked well. It was one of the most obvious story ideas you could have for the show — a character from the tunnel world witnessing a crime and then having to decide whether to expose his or her origins, where she lived, to see that justice is done in the world Above. That was a completely generic and obvious idea for the series, but I'm proud of the fact that we did it as a deaf girl and that we established this wonderful connection between Vincent and this girl. We took an extremely conventional idea and made it into something marginally special. When we were first watching dailies of Terrylene, those are moments I'm never going to forget. It's very special to have been a part of that show.

"It was also, if you recall, the first show in which there was another character in the tunnel world besides Father, Vincent and Kipper. The network had been deathly afraid of what was under there...dwarves, crippled people, and crazy lunatic homeless...they were just terrified by who we might populate the tunnel world with. So we didn't for a while, but we slowly started to do it. Then, George went crazy in 'Shades of Grey' and introduced all the tunnel characters."

Episode 1.12
"Shades of Grey"
Original Airdate: January 8, 1988
Written by George R.R. Martin and David E. Peckinpah
Directed by Thomas J. Wright
Guest Starring: David Greenlee (Mouse), Edward Albert (Elliot Burch), Cory Danziger (Kipper), Armin Shimerman (Pascal), Irina Irvine (Jamie), Joshua Rudoy (Eric), Kamie Harper (Ellie), James Avery (Winslow)

"Shades of Grey" trapped Vincent and Father in a cave, introduced a wide variety of tunnel dwellers and had Catherine have to go to Elliot Burch for equipment to help dig them out.

"This episode came about initially because of our budgetary problems," says George R.R. Martin. "We were running very badly over budget on a series of episodes. Frequently, the way you try to adjust this in television is to produce a cheap show called a bottle show. Locations and sets are one of the most expensive things to produce. David Peckinpah and I were basically teamed up and told that we should devise a bottle show to bring the budget down. It was originally called 'The Cave-In Show,' the idea being we can limit the amount of locations if we trap Vincent and someone in a cave-in and have them essentially stuck in one place for one show, playing out some character stuff. Should it be Vincent and Catherine? Should it be Vincent and Father? Should it be Vincent alone? Finally we arrived at Vincent/Father, with Catherine being instrumental in saving them.

"It didn't actually work that well as a bottle show," he laughs. "Even though a lot of it was limited to the cave-in, the actual chamber was not a standing set so we had to build that. The story required various other scenes up Above, in Catherine's office, in Elliot Burch's office and so forth. Unfortunately, it was not as big a help to our budgetary crisis as it might have been. However, I do think it turned out to be one of our strongest episodes. And it was a key episode. This was the point where we really broke through on the other people underground and the network dictate about that. We were able to use the bottle show budgetary thing to our advantage there. With Father and Vincent trapped in a cave-in, someone had to try and get them out. It couldn't be Kipper by himself. So that gave David and I the opportunity to introduce a whole bunch of new characters and really create the society underground. That was the episode where we first introduced Mouse, Winslow, Jamie and, I think, Mary. Alex and Howard had introduced the character Pascal in 'An Impossible Silence.'

"In many ways, it was one of the most important episodes of the first season. It established the underground world and it was the episode in which we brought back Elliot Burch and began the slow transformation of that character. David had originally introduced him in 'Siege' and that intrigued me. So, David and I discussed it and decided to bring the character back. I think Elliot, as played by Edward Albert, became a real asset to the development of the show. There was jeopardy in the episode, but it was also one of the first ones that got away without guys with guns that Vincent has to kill in the fourth act, which we were fighting desperately to stay away from. I think it established that you could do a dramatic and very effective show without having to resort to that kind of action/adventure format."

Alex Gansa states, "A fantastic episode, with a lot of good stuff between Father and Vincent. It introduced Mouse and a lot of other characters, and, again, more the way I envisioned the show. And some great stuff between Elliot Burch and Cathy. Elliot Burch was really George's baby. George really loved Elliot and treated him that way."

"Definitely a classic episode," concurs Howard Gordon. "What was good about that is that, for the first time, the underworld opened up and it helped to create the reality of Below."

Episode 1.13
"China Moon"
Original Airdate: January 15, 1988
Written by Cynthia Benjamin
Directed by Christopher Leitch
Guest Starring: Craig Ryan Ng (Yuehl), Phil Chon (Kuo), Keye Luke (Master), Jerry Tondo (Eddie), Rosalind Chao (Lin Wong), Vincent Wong (Dr. Wong), Dennis Dun (Henry Pei), James Hong (Chiang Lo Yi), Jeff Imada (Bruce)

Insert Catherine and Vincent into a modernized version of William Shakespeare's *Romeo and Juliet,* let it take place in New York's Chinatown and add a bit about the tunnels being invaded by Chinese warriors, and you've got the ingredients of "China Moon."

"Not one of my favorite episodes," says Howard Gordon. "There are certain conventions…the good twin-bad twin stories on all these science fiction shows, and you inevitably have your Chinatown episode. Like voodoo, Chinatown has got an atmosphere and a feeling and setting that is unfortunately used once, twice or three times in the course of any show. I think some of the Romeo and Juliet aspects of the story worked, but the Tongs, like in George's 'Terrible Savior,' were very broad villains who were more laughable than not when they descended into the tunnels with their weapons. Although I did like the last moment in that one, when Vincent kills the leader of the Tongs."

Adds Alex Gansa, "If you place certain episodes in certain categories, Vincent and Catherine helping lovers get together was a very important category for us. I think we had to rewrite that script in a day and a half and did some major work on it, which, again, is the nature of television. Because of budgetary concerns, you find yourself writing a substantial bulk of these things in an incredibly short amount of time, and the final product ultimately suffers somewhat. It was a fun episode and the wedding at the end was quite touching. Not one of my favorites, but certainly not a dog."

"No one was real enthused when we had to film that one," notes George R.R. Martin. "We were kind of approaching our last show of the first 13 and didn't have many scripts ready, and the ones we had we weren't too enthused about. We finally did 'China Moon' as the least of the evils, but I think it came together pretty well. I did a lot of work in terms of the action stuff at the end, and the whole fourth act is a big action sequence that I think works very well. I think it's one of the best action sequences we've ever done, playing it in the misty caverns with Vincent rising out of the mists and disappearing into the darkness, was very effective.

"We did get into some arguments toward the end of it with Standards and Practices, which was still on us first season. Their beef was the number of people that Vincent kills. He kills more people in that episode than he had killed before. In an earlier draft, he killed even more. I really think that network option on violence is hypocrisy of the rankest sort. I'm strongly opposed to sanitized television violence. If they want non-violent TV shows, that's great. I'd love to write more shows like 'Brothers,' 'Promises of Someday,' or any other non-violent, character-drama oriented shows that I did write. But you're always getting pressure from the network that they want what they call 'action,' which is the network code word for violence. Then, you give them action, and they want to tone it down. It's very clear that Vincent kills people, and we get this stupid note from Standards and Practices that said, 'It should not be clear that he is killing these people. He should have them destabilized.' That became a staff joke for the next three years, 'Vincent really destabilized that guy!' Right, he destabilized his head right off his shoulder. So, Vincent doesn't really kill the Chinese guys, he just destabilizes the shit out of them.

"And, in the climactic scene of that, when he's killed all these guys with their Ninja weapons, and he's facing the old man, that scene became a particular issue. There were actually two stages to that. The way I wanted it to go was essentially to have Vincent come in and the man says, 'Where are my other men?' And Vincent says, 'All dead,' which isn't in the final version. There, he doesn't say all dead, but, rather, 'None left.' Fresh out! Can't say that they're dead, even though they were screaming horribly as he killed them. Anyway, in the earlier draft he said 'All dead,' and the guy throws down his weapon and they have that whole dialogue, 'You wouldn't kill an unarmed man. You're the monster. I can see that part of you is a man of honor.' The Chinese warlord is essentially counting on the fact that Vincent is not going to kill him because he's unarmed. It was leading up to a sequence where Vincent says, 'What will you do if I let you go?' And he says, 'I'd come back with more men, better armed and better prepared. Only a monster would kill an unarmed man, and fortunately you are a man of honor.' In the original version, Vincent said, 'Only part of me is a man of honor, and the other part of me is not a man at all,' and he kills him! Great, but they wouldn't let us do it. The network hated it. Ron sort of liked that, because he always felt that part of Vincent is not a man, but he was a little nervous. It was early in the show's run, the end of the first 13. So we had to devise the whole thing with the Ninja guy coming up and flinging the star, because they wouldn't let us do that. It's really a pity, because the whole scene really leads to that, where, Vincent is saying that 'Part of me is a man, and part of me is the beast, you idiot!' The groundwork is laid earlier with the 'all men are demons when their loved ones are in danger' kind of thing.

"Then," Martin continues, "we had to do the ending where he's killed by the dying man's throwing star. In the first version of that ending, the throwing star catches the guy in the throat. Then, we get a note from Standards and Practices which says that the throwing star can't go in the throat. So, we ended up with the stupid throwing star in his chest, which will not kill you. Those little razor sharp edges are not long enough to get to the heart....they can't even get to the rib. Essentially, what we always say jokingly is that the old man was so shocked at getting stuck with the star, that he had a heart attack. To my mind, this dispute that took several back and forths, was a real case of the hypocrisy of the network's Standards and Practices. They weren't cutting down on the violence. They wanted us to kill this guy; no one suggested he should live. He was going to be killed with this throwing star, because they wouldn't let Vincent kill him, but it can't go in his throat because that might 'disturb' people. That might be too shocking, or something.

"To my mind, that's real bullshit. Death *should* disturb people. If there's one thing I'm proud of on *Beauty and the Beast* that we did, it was the fact that we may have been a violent show, but violence had consequences. Vincent didn't just kill people and go out with his other friends on the force and discuss the happy outcome of the case, like they do in so many cop shows. Did you ever see Starsky or Hutch or Hunter or any of these people bothered by the fact they just killed eight people? Death had consequences on *Beauty and the Beast* and I would like all death on television to have as much impact as real death does. Death is a shocking thing. We shouldn't trivialize it and make it an act break, and that's what the network wants you to do."

Episode 1.14
"The Alchemist"
Original Airdate: January 22, 1988
Written by Howard Gordon & Alex Gansa
Directed by Thomas J. Wright
Guest Starring: Tony Jay (Paracelsus), Ellen Geer (Mary), Albie Selznick (Zeke), Laura Harring (Carmen), Katherine Heard (Mary), Joey Aresco (Jimmy Morero), James Avery (Winslow)

This episode introduced underground villain Paracelsus (played by Tony Jay), once a friend of Father's, who was exiled from the community for his acts of evil. Now he resurfaces, selling a new and deadly drug to the world Above.

"A very strong episode," says Howard Gordon. "I think Tony Jay really took that episode away and was wonderful, and it really represented the first great antagonist we had. As we wrote the script, we had in mind that it had to be good, because we need to do a good, great villain. Of course, that was dependent on how it worked. In terms of the drug story, this is where reality kind of interfaces with fantasy. It was a fantasy drug, and it

THE LATE TONY JAY WAS CAST AS PARACELSUS, AN EPISODE GUEST STAR
WHO ENDED UP BECOMING AN INTEGRAL PART OF THE SERIES (PHOTO
COURTESY TONY JAY).

became a parable for drugs in general. I think it also met one of the challenges of the show by trying to interface the world Below with the world Above. When stories affected both worlds, I think that's also when we got some power."

Co-writer Alex Gansa notes that "The Alchemist" was "my personal favorite episode of them all. I just loved Paracelsus and I thought the whole drug thing was fantastic, and the relationship between Father and Paracelsus was great. Their scenes were evocative and spoke to a darkness we all carry around with us. For some reason, this worked for me on all cylinders. It just had an operable darkness about it that appeals to me on some levels. The action was extremely well shot.

"We wanted to create for Vincent the dual Father, the Luke-Darth Vader thing. We also wanted to create this schism in Vincent. He had this amazing, loving, sentimental, literary and romantic side, but he was a beast. We wanted to make it metaphorical that he had these two fathers, Jacob and John, and these were the two minds that were at work in forming his character at some level. One appealing to one side and one appealing to the other, and just lay the groundwork for that, which was built and torn down with agility at the end of the second season. This was the very, very beginning of that. I also think that kind of show promises a lot in the future. It gave us a villain for two seasons, and it promised some kind of struggle within Vincent which I was always fighting for. That's something I wanted to see brought forward a little more."

Guest Star Tony Jay recalls the episode fondly. "It was the introduction of Paracelsus, and I really feel it's one of the very best. They did a mystic thing there and introduced us to the enormous kind of invisibility of the character, establishing that he could disappear and come back in other forms. The allusion of the conjurer and the magician was there, so that stands out as well as this marvelous ambiance that they managed to get. Tom Wright directed that episode, and he is a marvelous director. He got the best out of it and I remember him saying, 'less….less…less,' and he got me down to almost the sheer presence of this evil man. Being a theater man, I'm inclined to go over the top a little, because it's a very different medium, but he got me down until it was just right. Then, of course, I based everything else on that assumption and they seemed to like it, so I kept with it."

Episode 1.15
"Temptation"
Original Airdate: February 5, 1988
Written by David E. Peckinpah
Directed by Gus Trikonis
Guest Starring: David Greenlee (Mouse), Jason Ross (Franklin), John Petlock *(Dr. Sanderle), Robert F. Hoy (Cassut), Carl Caifalio (Hopkins), Mark Schubb (Ted), Isabella Hofmann (Erika Salven), Milo O'Shea (Evan Brannigan), Herd Edelman (D.A. Levinson)*

To celebrate their first anniversary, Catherine and Vincent prepare gifts for each other, while Joe Maxwell is swept up in a relationship with a woman who is not what she seems to be in "Temptation."

"I didn't like the episode much," says David Peckinpah. "Koslow did the rewrite of that. Again, we were trying to see how the subsidiary characters would carry more weight. It worked for what it was, but by then I had gotten into a place of fury with Ron Koslow, and we weren't really communicating much. I was uncomfortable with the character of Vincent being so strong. I wanted him to have more vulnerability as far as being prone to human frailties. They leaned towards that later, but in the first season he was locked into this kind of Christ-like purity. It's awfully tough to write a character convincingly who doesn't have any flaws. Ron was just uncomfortable with any tension between the characters. But this is not to take away from the fact that *Beauty and the Beast* is Koslow's creation, and I think it will go down as one of the most innovative, fascinating programs done on TV."

Of the episode, director Gus Trikonis states, "I don't feel it was one of the better written shows. It was all right, but I didn't think it had the reach that some of the other stuff I eventually got to do had. I did get a chance to meet all the people at Witt-Thomas, solidify a relationship with Ron Koslow and meet with the actors. I loved working with Linda Hamilton. There was something so sensual about her. And all the actors were truly open to other actors and directors. There was a lot of sharing there. Perlman was terrific. I had a great time and was looking forward to doing more episodes."

Points out Howard Gordon, "'Temptation' was a bit of a disappointment. It was good to explore Joe and his life, and give him a love interest, but that was probably what would have been or should have been a second season episode. We weren't that far into the season and Joe was still a secondary character who the audience wasn't as interested in, as seeing something with Vincent and Catherine. From only that level, it was a disappointment. People seem to remember the completely incidental Catherine and Vincent aspect more than they remember or care about Joe's story. When the strongest memory of an episode is just a moment or two out of a whole episode, it leaves a lot to be desired."

Episode 1.16
"Promises of Someday"
Original Airdate: February 12, 1988
Written by George R.R. Martin
Directed by Thomas J. Wright
Guest Starring: John Franklin (Young Vincent), Andrew Held (Young Devin), Holly Sampson (Tomboy), Janet Cole Notey (Travel Clerk), Bruce Abbott (Devin Wells), Fred Lerner (Mounted Cop), Fred Dennis (Inspector), Max Battimo (Young Mitch)

As noted earlier, "Promises of Someday" reunited Vincent and Father with Devin, following a 20-year absence.

"My favorite of my first season episodes," enthuses George R.R. Martin. "It's a pure character drama. There's no action/adventure jeopardy in it whatsoever. There's some false jeopardy in the beginning in that you don't know if Devin is a good guy or a bad guy. I think it allowed us to see a little of Vincent's history. It was the first episode where we saw the young Vincent in flashback or mini-Vinnie, as we called him."

"Another great episode," says Alex Gansa. "I loved mini-Vinnie. George did a fantastic job. I thought the ending was a little convoluted and could have been streamlined a little more. That final scene between Devin and Father was a little too complicated, and there was too much going on between them to allow for any kind of real reconciliation or understanding."

Howard Gordon proclaims, "That one was a really excellent story. I think it was an amazing script, and it's one of those amazing things where I think the script wasn't done justice by the filming. It was a really beautifully written script. The fans really responded to Mini-Vinnie. Flashbacks are inherently undramatic because it doesn't push a story forward, but it's something that's used a lot on our show, and it's exciting to really discover the world and our characters in an earlier light."

Episode 1.17
"Down to a Sunless Sea"
Original Airdate: February 19, 1988
Written by Don Balluck
Directed by Christopher Leitch
Guest Starring: Cory Danziger (Kipper), Terri Hanauer (Jenny Aronson), Jim Meltzer (Steven Bass), Thomas Trujillo (Tony), Raymond Garcia (Hal), Marla Adams (Helen Thompson), Christine Jansen (Marcy O'Neill), Robert Cornthwaite (Morrison), Eric Poppick (Mercer)

"Down to a Sunless Sea" marks the return of Catherine's ex-fiancé, a man who remains psychotically obsessed with her.

"Someone told me that if Catherine falls in love with someone crazy again, he was going to kill himself," laughs Howard Gordon. "By that time she'd gotten involved with Elliot, who turned out to be a corrupt Nazi abusing concentration camp victims; she fell in love with the guy, who turned out to be a practitioner of voodoo; and now her ex-boyfriend was a murderer. It certainly makes one wonder about Catherine's judgment in men. Again, we're only up to episode 17. When she meets somebody and falls for him at some level, it really should be something special. This at least had the context of being her ex-lover, and it had some okay moments in it. It was very Hitchcockian, at least it set out to be Hitchcockian, and I'm not sure what we got. It didn't really add much to the show, although it was a fun challenge to get Vincent to the house to rescue her. Plus, Vincent again, really touching his rage, when he almost kills the guy."

Sighs Alex Gansa, "Oh God, let's move on. I just think when you work in television, you become an expert of the various incarnations of the homicidal maniac, and it is just so hard to pull off in 48 minutes of screenplay time, to make somebody with any kind of truth or believability. Ultimately, it turns out to be some kind of parody. Howard and I did a lot of work on that show, and it was not one of our best. We also overused the themes of Catherine falling in love and Vincent being jealous.

"It was because we were so constricted. Because these two could never be lovers, there were only a very finite number of powerful situations to put them in, in which the story revolved around them. One was Vincent being jealous of someone Catherine leaned on in a love way, there was Vincent kidnapped, there was Catherine kidnapped, and Vincent deciding that it would be better off if Catherine wasn't in his life, for her sake, or Catherine deciding that it would be better off if Vincent wasn't in her life, for his sake. That was it. What other stories could you tell? So, we gave her this progression of chinless men, as we called them, to fall in love with. You *could* think of a thousand different plots, but you couldn't think of ones that completely revolved around the relationship, because there was nowhere to go."

Episode 1.18
"Fever"
Original Airdate: February 26, 1988
Written by Mark Cassuett & Michael Cassutt
Directed by Thomas J. Wright
Guest Starring: Irvina Irvine (Jamie), Terri Hanauer (Jenny Aronson), Cory Danziger (Kipper), Ellen Geer (Mary), David Greenlee (Mouse), Kay E. Kuter (Alain Viso), Raye Birk (Edmonton), Alan Blumenfeld (Saul), David Clennon (Cullen), Stan Ivar (Jonathan Thorpe), James Avery (Winslow)

Greed from Above consumes the world of Below, when a treasure chest filled with gold is found on a newly discovered treasure ship in "Fever."

"I think 'Fever' is a very good episode and the most underrated one of the first season," comments George R.R. Martin, "and it produced one of the largest disputes between myself and Ron Koslow, and it produced some problems above with Tony Thomas. Tony didn't like the episode because too much of the story dealt with our secondary characters. He felt that we were losing Catherine and Vincent and he got kind of upset as he watched the dailies, because there were so many scenes in the tunnel community. One quote, and I was not present at these things so this is a fourth-hand quote, relayed to us is that Tony got quite angry and started yelling, 'Is this the Mouse and Winslow show? Are we going to change the title to that? What happened to *Beauty and the Beast*?' This may have factored into the killing of Winslow a couple of episodes later. The dispute between Koslow and me, which got quite acrimonious for a while, even though we ultimately did get past it, concerned the ending. The model for 'Fever' is basically *The Treasure of the Sierra Madre*.

"Thematically, the idea is that money is inherently corrupting, and the discovery of this treasure corrupts even the idyllic tunnel community. In the end, led by Vincent, they realize this, and chuck the money into the abyss. That was the final shot and, indeed, they were set up to do that final shot. We were like five days into the seven day shoot, but Ron had problems with that ending and finally imposed the 'give the treasure to the nuns' ending, which was shot very hastily and sort of tagged on at the end. Ron's argument was that it made our tunnel community look bad, so instead he had Vincent make this speech about how they should give the money to someone who could use it.

"I disagreed with that. My feeling is that we were saying worse things about the tunnel community when we give it away. What does it say here? It says that the tunnel community is morally flawed to handle this money in a sane way, but the nuns are somehow better, and it undercuts the whole thematic part of the money. Like in *Sierra Madre*, where the gold is blowing away in the wind, it's donated to a worthy cause. I think the irony of the situation and the whole thematic thrust required us to throw that money into the abyss. I feel that very strongly, and Ron felt very strongly the other way, and we got into some pretty strong arguments about this in the waning days. This was partially complicated by the fact that the episode's writers, Mark and Mike Cassutt, are good friends of mine. They're writers whose work I admired, their names are on that script and they felt that the treasure should be thrown into the abyss. That was their original vision. I thought this should be taken into account. Ron did not. He felt that the good of the show was more important than freelance writers. That became a very big argument, but, of course, it's his show, and he imposed his ending. I still feel that 'Fever' would be stronger with the other ending. It would be a darker, grimmer show, with a slightly different message.

"There was another change made along the way that I felt weakened it. There's a very key phrase in 'Fever' after Mouse has been stabbed by Colin. Jamie is saying, 'How can he do it? They were friends.' And Catherine says to her, 'It's a disease that comes from my world. It's called greed.' To my mind, that was a bad change. The original line illustrates what the episode is all about, which is the statement that all money -- *all money* -- is inherently corrupting. That a money-based society by its very nature is a corrupt society; and that our people in the utopian underworld who have a non-money-based society, a society based on human relations, interactions and people helping each other, have a superior society. By changing it to greed, it basically says, 'Well, there are some greedy people in the world.' I guess out there in Hollywood, people were just too afraid to speak that all money corrupts, because it's the main thing that drives the town. I think that change and the ending kind of weakened 'Fever,' though I still think it's a very strong episode."

Episode 1.19
"Everything is Everything"
Original Airdate: March 4, 1988
Written by Virginia Aldridge
Directed by Victor Lobl
Guest Starring: Cory Danziger (Kipper), Barbara Pilavin (Female Gypsy), Josh Blake (Tony Ramos), Robet Pastorelli (Vick Ramos), Will Kuluva (Milo Ramos), Renata Vanni (Eva Ramos), Jennifer Balgobin (Maria), Paul Greco (Joe)

Catherine and Vincent try to restore honor to a young gypsy boy's name and to bring him together with his dying grandfather in "Everything is Everything."

"This took me a little by surprise, because it felt very unlike the pilot," admits director Victor Lobl. "In flavor, it just felt very different from everything I've seen and everything I did subsequently. I don't have much memory of that script, except for the feeling that it had less to do with Catherine and Vincent than it did with the gypsy kid. There seems to be some confusion over the direction of the script, and that was never really worked out. We ended up with a script that was fun to shoot, everybody didn't take it terribly seriously and we went on from there."

"An episode I enjoyed a lot," says Howard Gordon. "We were lucky because we got a good actor to play the gypsy boy. We tried to do another story in New York that explored a different culture. We'd done Chinatown, and now we took on the gypsy culture. I think he was treated with some tenderness and some emotional truth to it."

George R.R. Martin points out, "It was sort of a fun episode. I always felt that B*eauty and The Beast* should have done more lighter episodes. But Hamilton really liked that episode. One of her things is that she always wanted to do more comedic episodes. She felt that she wanted to do comedy, and that she had a gift for it which the show didn't give her a chance to use. But let's face it; *Beauty and the Beast* was not good for a lot of the yucks. We essentially have a tragic situation, but I think a few creative moments and an occasional light episode can work. Not an out and out comedy like this one would have been good."

Episode 1.20
"To Reign in Hell"
Original Airdate: March 18, 1988
Written by Howard Gordon & Alex Gansa
Directed by Christopher Leitch
Guest Starring: Ellen Geer (Mary), Tony Jay (Paracelsus), Beah Richards (Narcissa), Armin Shimerman (Pascal), Irina Irvine (Jamie), James Avery (Winslow), John Minton (Erlik)

Paracelsus returns to kidnap Catherine in "To Reign in Hell." He takes her to the bowels of the underworld and Vincent, accompanied by Pascal and Winslow, must rescue her, facing possible death in the process.

"A tribute to any and all of the quest myths," says Howard Gordon, "but a huge disappointment to me personally. An original idea was that Paracelsus left a bent gold coin in Catherine's apartment for Vincent to find. That gold coin was supposed to be the passage across a river Below. There was a whole scene with the Waterman, the gatekeeper. We had laid in so much stuff leading up to this Waterman. Quests go from point-to-point and things bleed into each other and in that scene a lot of stuff was illuminated that remained completely unilluminated in the final cut. That missing scene made the story a little bit more intricate and elegant."

Alex Gansa concurs with Gordon's assessment of the episode. "It was an episode that suffered because of its ambitions," he notes. "We had envisioned a very mythic journey for Vincent to free Catherine from Paracelsus, and it turned a little campy. The screenplay was far superior to what turned out on the television and ultimately it was a failed episode. We just didn't have the time to do what was written. We had to cut out a lot of scenes and of course there was the much-debated Winslow death that split the staff right down the middle. People wouldn't talk to each other for days after that. Somebody had to die, because we had lost all the expensive scenes and we needed some emotion, so in true *Beauty and the Beast* fashion, we cut off somebody's head.

"Death was one of our staples," he adds with a laugh. "I feel that only insofar that stories were so hard to come up with for that show, and the interface between the two worlds became a tricky problem, that we ultimately succumbed to killing off beloved characters as a way of generating some emotion."

George R.R. Martin explains that "To Reign in Hell" was not one of his favorite episodes. "The big dispute in that, of course, was the killing of Winslow. Alex and Howard were doing that show and it was designed as a classic quest. From Joseph Campbell or somebody else, they had gotten this notion that a quest had to contain a meaningful death, so they decided that Winslow should be the one to die. David Peckinpah and I created Winslow in 'Shades of Grey,' and we had plans for that character. He was a necessary character, he fulfilled a good function on the Council, James Avery was a superb actor who played him very well, he was a good sympathetic black character, which I thought was nice to have in the mix; and we *didn't* want him to die. So Peckinpah and I fought like demons to prevent this. We didn't really attack the boys' notion of wanting a meaningful death, we just said, 'Why don't you kill Pascal?'

"So, essentially, it became us suggesting that Pascal be killed and the boys insisting on it being Winslow, because they had created Pascal and had plans for that character. Of course, they had the inside track there, because they were actually writing the episode. Koslow was initially neutral, but at the same time 'To Reign in Hell' was being written, 'Fever' was being filmed and that's where the incident with Tony Thomas occurred where he expressed displeasure at seeing so much of Mouse and Winslow in that episode. Evidently that kind of swung Koslow around and he said, 'Winslow's got to die,' so at that point it was lost. Avery was a real addition to the show. Peckinpah and I went into Koslow's office after we saw some of the dailies, before they were supposed to shoot the death scene, and made an impassioned plea, 'Don't kill this character. Have him seriously wounded and he has to go back. You don't have to kill anyone.' But it failed. I still think it was unfortunate.

"In a way, 'To Reign in Hell' and my second season episode, 'Dead of Winter,' inspired a little bit of the trilogy [that concluded season two] simply because it left open certain areas, if you think about it. In 'To Reign in Hell,' why the hell did any of these things happen this way? Paracelsus says he wants is to kill Vincent, but if he wants to kill Vincent, why send a giant to kidnap Catherine and bring her way below the earth so that Vincent will come after her so that the giant can fight him? Why not station the giant in a place where Vincent is going to be passing? We didn't really address that in the episode, but it did cause us to think later. Paracelsus can't *really* want to kill Vincent, because he's not going about it very efficiently. He wants something else. What is it? That led to the exploration of Paracelsus' past and all that. We were all excited about 'To Reign in Hell' when the boys started work on it, because it was such a mythic and fantastic show, but I don't think anybody was entirely thrilled with the way it turned out."

On returning as Paracelsus, Tony Jay states, "That episode showed Paracelsus is a man of learning, because he quotes Milton: 'It is better to reign in Hell than to serve in Heaven.' That shows he was a learned man, and also gave us some samples of his quirky humor. He was very amused by things. That was nice and very good, compounding his threat and the menace when he steals Cathy. The nice thing is that Parcelsus escapes once more."

David Peckinpah doesn't agree. "The show started to become more science fiction and fantasy oriented and it lost its reality handhold along the way," he opines. "As soon as the Paracelsus thing started, I thought it became very cult-like. When it started to become the world below the world Below, it really started losing its accessibility for the mainstream audience. Albeit the basic concept is very weird, but then it took mythology to places previously unseen on network TV and people weren't ready for it."

Episode 1.21
"Ozymandias"
Original Airdate: April 1, 1988
Written by George R.R. Martin
Directed by Frank Beascoechea
Guest Starring: Bill Marcus (D.A. Moreno), Edward Albert (Elliot Burch), David Greenlee (Mouse), Carl Strano (Roth), Alexander Folk (Guard), Gerald Castillo (Simons), Linda Porter (Elizabeth)

In "Ozymandias," Elliott Burch plans on breaking ground for a new skyscraper, which will expose the world Below. Catherine agrees to marry him in order to prevent its construction.

George R.R. Martin says, "Another Elliott Burch episode. Even though David Peckinpah created the character, by 'Ozymandias' I became the guardian of Elliot Burch and ended up doing a great many of the Elliot Burch episodes including this one. I don't think it came out quite as strongly as it should have. Originally, when I first saw it I was kind of disappointed, but as I've seen it over and over, I think it's actually better than I had first thought. Edward Albert was very sick during the filming of that, but despite that he did a good job. I think Elliot worked well for us. In all of my fiction, I've always been fascinated by characters that have shades of grey within themselves. That's part of the fascination of Vincent, too. He's not simply the Hero. He does have a dark side to him and that gives you a lot to work with."

"Another really nice story involving Elliot Burch," says Howard Gordon. "It, too, originally had a different slant. That was a story that Alex and I were originally going to do. It was called 'The Tower' when we were developing it, but George took the ball and ran with it, coming up with a much better story than the one we had. It was probably the episode that really spoke to what Elliot was about, providing more depth to this secondary character."

Episode 1.22
"A Happy Life"
Original Airdate: April 8, 1988
Written by Ron Koslow
Directed by Victor Lobl
Guest Starring: Mimi Craven (Rebecca), Caryn West (Mom), Marina Suriano (Jill), Patrick Pankhurst (Paul), Kelly Kehoe (Young Cathy), Zachary Benjamin (Jeremy), Turley Travis (Kay), Annette McCarthy (Jenny), John McMartin (Charles Chandler), Betsy Brantley (Nancy Tucker)

The season concluded with "A Happy Life," in which Catherine and Vincent come to grips with the true depth of their feelings, culminating in the long awaited kiss...sort of.

Says Alex Gansa, "One of the supremely popular episodes, and another example of Koslow's genius, as far as I was concerned. The show was really about Vincent and Catherine, and those shows are always our strongest episodes. It was a very, very romantic, powerful show, and probably the kind of show we should have been doing more of. But, again, it was hard creating crises between our two lead characters all the time."

Director Victor Lobl reflects, "That's where I discovered Linda's potential as an actress. Linda and I had worked together previously on a show called *King's Crossing*, and she was one of three girls and it was hard to ascertain anyone's capabilities. All three girls were pretty young and they were sort of stretching their muscles. In 'Everything is Everything,' the script was fairly light for her and for Ron, so there was nothing really for me to gauge. I could see she was professional and I knew she was a good actress. I thought she was brilliant in *Terminator*, one of those weird films that really took me by surprise. In 'Happy Life,' the material seemed personally probing for her. It was a very delicate, careful process which was very gratifying, because you don't have many opportunities that are rich enough or provide such resonance for an actor. It was a particularly gratifying experience, because we got to know how to work with each other, and that really set up our relationship for the rest of the show's run."

"Koslow's magic," smiles Howard Gordon. "Ron has the uncanny ability to take what might seem flat on the page and have it come out great on the screen. He really had a connection to the Catherine/Vincent relationship that I don't think anyone really matched. Of course, it had the controversial kiss, and there is footage of them kissing like Gable and Lombard. But it really turned out to be something that the network, and even us at some level, were frightened about. Maybe we wimped out, but at the same time I would have ultimately voted for a more subtle approach. Maybe a little bit more, maybe I would rather have seen a tender kiss, but I think tongues just would have been too much."

George R.R. Martin clarifies, "They filmed the ending with a kiss and without the kiss, and came to some sort of compromise. What we kept hearing about the kiss is that once it happens, the show's over. But that's too literal an interpretation of the original model. In the original *Beauty and the Beast*, once they kiss it *is* over, because the kiss symbolically represents what turns him back into human form. For us, there was a lot more to explore beyond the kiss."

At that stage, the show was most definitely not over, with everyone — including the critics and the public — judging the first season a success.

"I think we did some good work in all three seasons, and I think we got better as the first season went along," points out Martin. "We got to know the characters more and wrote things that were more interesting. Of course, we were going very well in the ratings at that time, typically winning our timeslot. We came in first throughout most of the first season and that gave us the license to experiment and try some different things. The first season ended with 'A Happy Life,' which I think the fans are pleased by. It was a very strong and romantic way to wrap up the first season."

"You're always in the middle of it and you always have discontents," says Howard Gordon, "but I think, in hindsight, it was really the golden time. Part of it, too, was the newness of it – creating the characters and discovering them. That's the excitement for a writer. Things like the underworld, which the network was afraid to explore. It was kind of a forbidden fruit. They were always telling us it was crazy and it wouldn't work, but were elated by the thing. There were some embarrassing things too; I think the writing on the second season may have been better. There were good ones and bad ones. It's kind of like having a batting average. If you can hit two or three really good episodes in a season, you've done well for yourself."

Alex Gansa believes that the first season was the show's best. "Without a doubt," he states. "A lot of things factor into my saying that. Mostly because we were so new, all the avenues of storytelling were open to us, which became stale in the second and third years. We were at the beginning and were all playing our best game. We were all a thousand percent behind the show, extremely excited; people were at their creative highpoint. For those reasons, I'll always look back on that first year as an amazing season, filled with our own kind of adventure and excitement."

THERE WAS A FEELING ON STAFF THAT A CERTAIN FAMILIARITY HAD
CREPT INTO THE VINCENT AND CATHERINE RELATIONSHIP WHICH WAS
ULTIMATELY DEEMED DETRIMENTAL TO THE SHOW (PHOTO: CBS).

SEASON TWO

Although season two of *Beauty and the Beast* was delayed until November of 1988 due to that year's Writer's Guild Strike, Ron Koslow was confident that the show would become a bigger hit as the new batch of episodes would be exploring themes the show's fans had grown to love.

"There is a reason this relationship is, shall we say, charged," he explained to the media. "There is an implicit taboo, an implicit impossibility to this relationship. I think any time you have that kind of electricity between two people, it's far more interesting to explore that power than to attempt to neutralize it. I think we're going to see a deeper communication between the two of them; we hope to deepen the relationship and to explore it a bit more, that perfect but impossible relationship. The viewers do seem to be quite drawn to Vincent and Catherine, and, frankly, it's something that continues to fascinate us as writers. These are two people who in many ways can be closer on a very fundamental level than most people — two people who can be completely honest with each other. What we want to do is explore the implications of that honesty."

He noted that advantage would be taken of both the underworld and New York. "There's a whole civilization down there, a utopian world beneath the streets of New York. Who are they? How did they get there? What are they *doing* down there? To me, New York is also a magical place. New York is the primeval forest of our time, full of wonders and terrors. In New York, you can turn a corner, run into someone, and your life can change. We want to explore that — but always in the context of this epic romance."

Linda Hamilton also expressed enthusiasm over the first batch of episodes shot for year two. "The show has taken a turn," she said. "We've done six episodes in which Catherine hasn't beaten up anybody. That behavior doesn't make me like the show very much. Now I get to waltz onscreen and deal with great issues of the heart, live as a New York City career woman, wear great clothes. Catherine's got the best of both worlds. It's important not to get lost in one type of behavior. That's what formula television does."

Ironically, the approach that Hamilton was praising was, in a sense, dooming the show.

Episode 2.1
"Chamber Music"
Original Airdate: November 18, 1988
Written by Ron Koslow
Directed by Victor Lobl
Guest Starring: David Greenlee (Mouse), Ellen Geer (Mary), Dion Basco (Paco), Terrance Ellis (Rolley, Age 18), Garland Spencer (Rolley, Age 11), Janet MacLachlan (Miss Kendrick), Shavar Ross (Anthony), Theodore Bikel (Eli)

The second season of *Beauty and the Beast* began with "Chamber Music," in which Catherine and Vincent attempt to help a former tunnel dweller piano prodigy overcome a dependency on drugs.

Alex Gansa says, "It's amazing how you can deceive yourself. I remember seeing that episode and saying, 'This is just great.' It was real, it seemed to have a lot of emotion and it was a beautifully written, shot and scored episode. Unfortunately, it wasn't about Catherine and Vincent, which was our problem. I think because of its ambiguous ending and Vincent wasn't ultimately successful in resurrecting this drug addict's life, it was a downer and probably the wrong foot to get off on."

George R.R. Martin differs, "I thought it was gutsy the way it ended. A nice piece, though not particularly a Catherine/Vincent story, but I thought it was one of Ron Koslow's strongest scripts. The Rolley character was a nice one, and the ending was a particularly heart-wrenching ending, which didn't offer any easy answers. Again, we were trying to not be television, we were trying to be true and the truth is that a junkie doesn't necessarily give up dope because somebody gives him a moving lecture."

"I really liked that episode a lot, " points out Howard Gordon, "but my only hindsight disappointment is the fact that it didn't deal with 'A Happy Life' at all. The first scene is of them enjoying this incredibly tender moment Below in a way we'd never seen them before. There was always this tension between them; there was always this distance and impossibility. But suddenly between summer hiatus, they had been holding hands and just going to concerts. Before that the feeling I had was the only time they saw each other is when we saw them. Here somehow, we got the intimation that they're going to concerts, they're going to movies together. While that was very sweet and tender, that was kind of the underpinning of the slackening of tension. Otherwise, it was a very nice episode, and I remember the critics even liked that we were not afraid to show a dark story."

Victor Lobl relates that "Chamber Music" was "My most enjoyable experience in television, period. The boy who played Rolley [Terrance Ellis] was a lovely young actor. Occasionally, I have a really special experience with very young actors. They fall in love with the whole process and you see them take everything in as though it's a family and they become very committed, very involved and very connected to this family. It's really sort of bittersweet to see them pull away from it at the end. It's a very powerful experience for them and you get to remember why you're doing this in the first place. I thought he was wonderful for me to work with, very responsive and we had fun visually with it, making it look as though he were really playing the piano. I was very happy with that show. There were a lot of small touches I put in there that I was happy with, and we took the time to do some unusual things."

Episode 2.2
"Remember Love"
Original Airdate: November 25, 1988
Written by Virginia Aldridge
Directed by Victor Lobl
Guest Starring: David Greenlee (Mouse), Tony Jay (Paracelsus), Irina Irvine (Jamie), Armin Shimerman (Pascal), Nicholas Hormann (Tom Gunther)

Vincent imagines what life would have been like for his loved ones without him. The alternate reality is not a pleasant one in this episode, which some have termed "It's a Wonderful Vincent."

"Again, a very dark story," emphasizes George R.R. Martin. "The world without Vincent was a very dark place indeed. Some of it, frankly, pushed it. In the model you're working with, *It's a Wonderful Life*, everything was a little more logical. Assuming that Father would be a bum in the gutter if Vincent doesn't exist pushes it to a certain extent. Even if you say the baby Vincent was such a great inspiration…well, okay, but I don't know."

Victor Lobl points out, "On the set, everyone was uncomfortable at how similar this was to *It's a Wonderful Life*. There was a slightly awkward feeling about that, but from moment to moment, everyone tried to have fun. The actors, Ron in particular, were unhappy about that one, and there were many, many nights of long dialogue changes. We reshot some of it, removed some of it. I was never really happy with it. For me, what that was, more than anything else, an exercise in the use of simple camera tricks."

Howard Gordon explains, "This one was supposed to be the season opener. Virginia Aldridge came in and told us this story, and when she finished, we all stood up and applauded, which is the first time that happened. What I think ultimately turned out disappointing about it is that if you're going to do a take-off on *It's a Wonderful Life*, something has to be more interesting. It really was derivative and there was no masking that. For instance, when *Moonlighting* did it, everybody is better off without Maddie. I don't think we made it interesting enough to warrant the derivation.

"I also think the motivation was ill-conceived. The original story had it that one of the children Below was an autistic child, who ends up dying.

For whatever combination of reasons, we didn't follow through with that, and did something that I think ultimately weakened the motivations for his self-doubt. Plus, something that other people have pointed out, in his grief, Vincent smashes the stained glass window by his bed and collapses to the floor. He wakes up in this 'wonderful life' world, and when he wakes up in reality, the stained glass window is intact again. George bitched about it from the beginning and we said, 'Ah, it's just a dream. Don't worry about it.' But people called us on it, and I think George was right."

"More than anybody I think I was responsible for this episode, and more than anybody I think I should hoist myself up by the ankles," laughs Alex Gansa. "It just seemed like such a good idea at the time. Instead of putting an interesting twist or commenting on the model, or using it as a point of reaction, it just used the model too exclusively. It was a rip-off instead of a comment on *It's a Wonderful Life*. As far as I was concerned, a very unsuccessful episode and not creatively inspired."

Reportedly, this episode marked dissension in the writing staff, as some members wanted to use this particular story as an excuse to drive a wedge between the Vincent/Catherine relationship, while others thought it was a bad idea.

"It would have influenced the whole course of the season," says a staff member. "The feeling was quite similar to what had been going on in *Star Trek: The Next Generation*; the feeling that you didn't want animosity or trouble between these two characters. That was always resisted at the higher levels of the show. People really wanted there to be a strong love connection. That's fine for the end of the fairy tale, but you have a real tough time retaining any sort of dramatic tension throughout the year with Vincent and Catherine being so symbiotic; drama is conflict."

Episode 2.3
"Ashes, Ashes"
Original Airdate: December 2, 1988
Written by Alex Gansa & Howard Gordon; Story by Roy Dotrice
Directed Gus Trikonis
Guest Starring: David Greenlee (Mouse), Zachary Rosencrantz (Zach), Irina Irvine (Jamie), Ellen Geer (Mary), Carolyn Finney (Rita Escobar), Joseph Campanella (Dr. Peter Alcott), Kamie Harper (Ellie), Adrian Paul (Dmitri Benko), Joshua Rudoy (Eric), Tony Maggio (Sammy)

A defecting Russian sailor reaches the underworld, bringing a deadly plague with him in "Ashes, Ashes."

"Another death Below, this time Ellie. We were getting very somber," observes Alex Gansa. "It was an idea that had been bouncing around the previous season, this idea of 'What would happen if some sort of medical disaster took place down there? How responsible would Father feel, because their medical supplies and technique are so limited and how culpable would he be if somebody kicked the bucket?' So, those were issues we'd been throwing around. Ultimately, it was a pretty successful episode.

"I think Ellie's death was handled well, and it showed how devastated people were, how much they really cared about that society down there. Anytime we could divide that community over an issue like this, it was obviously good. At the same time, this was an episode that was probably too somber and too removed from Vincent and Catherine to be one of the real seminal episodes of the series."

Adds Howard Gordon, "That was an idea inspired by Roy Dotrice. It was really a dark show in that you had kids dying, and I think at that point you had fans saying, 'What is going on?' Our darker sides were coming out, although I think the stories were really well told and there were some very tender moments, but that was the beginning to dominate the tone of the series and I think that in broad terms that was not a good thing. You don't want to get too depressed. I was really a fan of the writing and the way the whole episode was executed."

"Very dark," concurs George Martin, "but a powerful episode. We brought back the kids from 'A Children's Story' and killed Ellie and made Eric the dramatic focus of it. That was a case where the script evolved, and I think evolved in the direction of greater dramatic truth. In the early version of the story, as Roy envisioned it, Dimitri dies, everyone else gets sick and Father gets sick, and there's some suspense, 'Is Father going to die?' As we developed the story, we got to talking about it and it's just so television to say, 'Okay, Father gets sick, is Father going to die?' Who's going to really believe that they're going to kill Father? So, he recovers at the end, and everybody recovers at the end. The truth is that when people get these terrible diseases, sometimes they die. You can't just work hard and get everybody better. We thought that was an interesting direction to take the story in."

Director Gus Trikonis says, "This one was Roy Dotrice's concept, and I had a terrific time on the show because he was there all the time, watching his brainchild come to life. From day to day, we worked on the material and brought more to it. I thought the story was an interesting one, a real tearjerker. But the overall series had that sense to it."

Episode 2.4
"Dead of Winter"
Original Airdate: December 9, 1988
Written by George R.R. Martin
Directed by Victor Lobl
Guest Starring: David Greenlee (Mouse), Irina Irvine (Jamie), Ellen Geer
(Mary), Tony Jay (Paracelsus), Beah Richards (Narcissa), Armin Shimerman
(Pascal), Marcie Leeds (Samantha), Ritch Brinkley (William), Philip Waller
(Geoffrey), Joseph Campanella (Dr. Peter Alcott), Clive Rosengren (Lou), Kathryn
Spitz (Rebecca), Tony Steedman (Sebastian), Anne Haney (Tamara)

"Dead of Winter" chronicles the Winterfest holiday celebrated by the
people Below, and Paracelsus' attempts to disrupt that celebration. It is an
episode that the majority of *B&B* fans took to heart.

"At some point during the first season, we somehow had gotten around
to talking about festivals and holidays Below, and wondered whether they
have any of their own," explains George R.R. Martin. "There's a reference in
the first season episode, I think it was 'Fever,' where Colin is making a chess
set, and it was a gift for Father at Winterfest. I started debating what that
should be like. What's the purpose of it? I came up with the notion of a fes-
tival to honor the helpers, which Ron liked a lot. So when we were talking
about our first episodes of that year, Ron encouraged me to write that show.

"'Dead of Winter' was another of our — or my, George R.R. Martin's —
budget busters. I have a reputation, unfortunately well deserved, for writing very expensive episodes that drive the crew crazy and push them beyond
things we've done before. I never really realized that Winterfest was that. I
said, 'Hey, it's going to be easy, because 80% takes place in this one room.'
Well, the one room was a new set, the Great Hall, which was the biggest set
we ever built. It had to be quite large. The amount of extras and actors we
had to hire to fill out the cast and give a sense of the Winterfest was very
large. So, 'Dead of Winter' has the largest set and the largest cast of any of
our shows, and was the most expensive and all that. Big party scenes are
very, very expensive to shoot and very difficult to direct. Victor Lobl really
had a challenge there. It was the only episode — of our early episodes —
that had a strong action adventure element to it in that Paracelsus infiltrates
Winterfest and plans on blowing things up.

"Everybody else at that stage, at the beginning of second season, was
writing character-oriented pieces. At the same time I was working on
'Winterfest,' Ron was working on 'Chamber Music,' the boys were doing
'God bless the Child' and David Peckinpah was working on a script called
'The Prodigal,' which was never filmed, but had the return of Mitch Denton.
P.K. Simonds had joined the staff and was working on a script that became
'A Fair and Perfect Night.' So, these were relatively slow scripts, and I decided

that 'Winterfest' should have some harder elements. It was also the show to introduce Paracelsus' ability to mimic voices and assume people's faces. To a certain extent, with Paracelsus I was building on things that Alex and Howard had introduced in 'To Reign in Hell,' the sense of him as a ruler of another underground kingdom far, far Below. There were also hints of his backstory and things we would pick up and explore later. In this confrontation with Father, he makes reference to some secret between them; something Father remembers one way and he remembers another. So, we were gradually beginning to learn more about the character, his motivations, his history, about Vincent's past. Oddly enough, I think the elements that the fans react to most in 'Dead of Winter' is not any of these plot or action elements, but the whole notion of the Winterfest celebration and a sense of togetherness. It's not an episode that I think was beloved by the network. It was never rerun by them."

Alex Gansa explains, "Again, it was a question of a far too ambitious script, although I think this one came off a thousand times more successfully than 'To Reign in Hell.' We did learn from the fact that if you build things on too grand a scale, they're going to come off a little cheesy on a little box, especially if you're forced to cut corners. I think this was an example of a script that was far better than the final product. But it was very inventive, and George is a master at that kind of thing. That's an episode that Howard and I wouldn't go near with a 10-foot pole, because it was done on a much larger scale and dealt with a lot of people. George tended to play bigger, broader themes, while Howard and I tended to play to smaller, more human themes. Which was a good diversity to have on staff, and we helped each other out in that way."

"Another George R.R. Martin/Cecil B. De Mille classic," reflects Howard Gordon. "If I could characterize George's stories, he thought in these epic, $20 million terms, whereas Alex and I thought smaller, with more personal stories. If you look over the episodes, our stories tend to be about hookers, deaf girls and things like that. George's tended to be about Winterfest and that kind of thing. 'Dead of Winter' was a huge organizational and budgetary fiasco, building this great hall and everything. But all in all, I think it was a lot of fun. I think the moment that everyone lives for is when Catherine and Vincent waltz at the end. It's just an incredibly tender moment. The fans just loved it, and I loved it.

"From the very beginning of *Beauty and the Beast*, we've wondered if Vincent and Catherine would ever dance. Some fans felt they were cheated, like they were with the kiss, which was done in shadow. I wanted to remain as evocative as possible. What remains unseen is ultimately the most enticing, so I loved that moment. For me, again, if we did two or three episodes that were good, and if you have one moment in the show that's memorable, I think you've really done more than an episode of *Jake and the Fatman*."

Victor Lobl looks upon this episode as the biggest production effort of the series. "Just a lot of people packed into the underground hall," he says, "which was shot in something like four days. Television restrictions to get some of those effects work on time, within the hours you've got, was very demanding. And we had a very exhausted crew by the end of the shoot. We also had a fabulous time, because there was a party atmosphere. In fact, half of the shoot was in this party area and it was, in fact, a party. There was food, people were carrying on as though it were a party they had all been invited to and had somehow gotten stuck in a room for four days. When we came to the end of that show, it felt like the end of the season. When we wrapped it, there was a kind of bittersweet relief for everyone. There was hugging and kissing and people saying goodbye, but then we had to crank it up right away. That's a typical George Martin situation. Every time I got hit with one of his scripts, which were fun to work with, I knew that we were going to have heavy, heavy hours. They always had deceptively simple sequences which in truth were very tough to shoot.

"The fans really seem to love that show because there's so much stuff going on. You kind of get the feeling you've discovered something that nobody knows, because it seems like throwaway background. We had an opportunity to do some things that set it up with depth, and that was a lot of fun."

George R.R. Martin adds, "This was the period where we realized we had some difficulties. Because of the Writers Strike, the whole season was delayed. We had this notion that each year we would do a Halloween episode and it would become one of our staples. The annual *Beauty and the Beast* Halloween episode was something we never seemed to get. During the first season, we actually managed to be on right on Halloween, but the second year, the Writers Strike delayed everything and we couldn't get on the air until mid-November. Unfortunately, sitcoms are much easier to get up to speed than dramatic shows, so ABC had sitcoms on six weeks ahead of us. And, to my mind, that was a really damaging blow. By the time we came on, they were really very well established and getting good ratings, and we never won the timeslot again. Our first season victories were gone and now we were finishing a distant second. Our actual ratings were not much different than they had been first season, but our share was down. Second is different than first, and towards the end of the second season, we would dip down to third occasionally, which is not too good as far as the network is concerned. Of course, we didn't know that at the beginning of the second season, when we were writing and producing the shows. We were a little naïve, or certainly optimistic, that we would come back on the air and our fans would return and we would be the number one show.

"I think in retrospect, that we may have returned to the second season the wrong way. In the wave of shows we opened the season with — 'Chamber Music,' 'Ashes, Ashes,' 'Dead of Winter,' 'God Bless the Child' — there were no real strong action shows among them. I don't think Vincent really beasts out in any of those shows. They were predominantly very dark in tone, a slower pace and more character oriented. Some of them really are quite dark. I think the audience that came back after the summer was expecting a more romantic follow-up to 'A Happy Life.'"

Episode 2.5
"God Bless the Child"
Original Airdate: December 16, 1988
Written by Howard Gordon & Alex Gansa
Directed by Gus Trikonis
Guest Starring: Marcie Leeds (Samantha), Ellen Geer (Mary), Zachary Rosencrantz (Zach), Katy Boyer (Lena), Willard E. Pugh (Maurice)

A former prostitute falls in love with Vincent in "God Bless the Child."

"A show I really liked, and one in which we lucked out with the casting," admits Howard Gordon. "A parable, really, a Christmas story. One of my favorite stories, although a lot of fans were offended by Lena as a kind of Mary Magdalene character. There's sort of a likening similarity between Vincent and Jesus Christ, which was totally unintentional, but people certainly latched onto it. There's certainly a lot read into it, but if there's an argument to be made, then it's legitimate, I guess."

Notes Alex Gansa, "I think we had one of our best guest stars, and the show itself I thought was quite sweet. It was a Christmas show and meant to be hopeful. On staff, it was a real favorite, but we struggled with the problem on staff of 'To what extent would this person drive a wedge between Catherine and Vincent?' Howard and I thought it should be a significant threat, to make it really call their relationship into question — the fact that there's somebody else who loves Vincent at some level. Unfortunately, as far as I was concerned, and who knows if it was the right decision or not, that aspect of the show got watered down and, ultimately, that made it a lesser episode than it might have been. But still, I hold a special place in my heart for that episode."

Adds George R.R. Martin, "I don't have much to say about it, but I think it's a great episode, probably the boys' best episode. We were really hitting on our casting there, and our guest star gave an extraordinary performance."

"One of my favorite shows," reflects Gus Trikonis. "When I would read the material, there were moments that Howard and Alex would write in their description that touched me unconsciously and consciously, stirring up images. That never quite happened before, and that's why I feel 'God Bless the Child' really did something special for me as a director. Every day would become more enhanced by the day before. It was truly a special time. The post-production crew had done more with it than I had. Normally with producers, they usually take the material you give them and sort of take something out of it, whereas in this case they added something to it. It was truly a unique experience for me.

"The whole relationship between the girl and Vincent touched me. She saw beyond his face and when she went to his bed, he shunned her, told her to leave. He had his own inner turmoils and passions which were starting to work on him. It was one of those times when he actually could have conflict in his relationship with Catherine. I felt all of that working in the material, and the actors were all there with that also."

Episode 2.6
"Sticks and Stones"
Original Airdate: January 6, 1989
Written by Howard Gordon & Alex Gansa
Directed by Bruce Malmuth
Guest Starring: Ritch Brinkley (William), William C. Byrd (Miguel), Diane Dorsey (Woman), Jack Burns (Hose), Terrylene (Laura Williams), Ed Kelly (Lincoln), Charles Bouvier (Sgt. Greg McQueeney), Kathryn Spitz (Rebecca), Ron Marquette (Jerry), Warren Munson (Willis), Tim Russ (Lt. Eric Parker)

Former underground resident Laura ("An Impossible Silence") falls in with a dangerous deaf street gang in "Sticks and Stones," an episode which features an unprecedented scene between deaf people without sound.

"The best directed episode we ever did," believes Alex Gansa. "It was a very spontaneous job behind the camera, and I think the energy of that shows on screen. I think there's a lot of energy and a lot of real tension and passion floating around in that episode. This episode can be put in the same category as 'God Bless the Child' and 'Brothers': they're mostly about a guest star. I just don't think that was serving us as well as it might have, only because we didn't let those things reflect on the relationship of Catherine and Vincent as much as we should have. Although I love Terrylene, and I think she's absolutely fantastic and the idea of a deaf gang was really cool, as was really trying to get into the deaf culture. It was a wild chance that paid off and got us a lot of publicity. I just think we were straying away from our bread and butter, which was a mistake. I thought it looked great, it was extremely violent — which was a welcome change for us on that level — and I ultimately thought it was a successful episode."

Adds Howard Gordon, "I think we really pushed the issue of deafness. Apparently, it had not been done when there were scenes played out between and among deaf actors. The fear was, 'Will people pay attention?' For the first time, we wanted to put the audience in the place of deaf people who are subjected to close captioning. We had an ensemble of deaf actors, all of whom were tremendous, and I think that episode worked quite well. It had a little *West Side Story/Romeo and Juliet* aspect, and it worked well."

Episode 2.7
"A Fair and Perfect Knight"
Original Airdate: January 13, 1989
Written by P.K. Simonds, Jr.
Directed by Gus Trikonis
Guest Starring: Zachary Rosencrantz (Zach), Marcie Leeds (Samantha), Ellen Geer (Mary), Laurel Moglen (Brooke), Philip Waller (Geoffrey), Bill Calvert (Michael), Cyd Strittmatter (Beth), Riad (Tina)

In "A Fair and Perfect Knight," a friend of Vincent's, Michael, goes to live in the world Above, and it seems as though something is happening between he and Catherine, which fills Vincent with jealousy.

"Interesting episode and very challenging in many ways," explains P.K. Simonds, Jr. "You kind of look at the impossibility of Catherine and Vincent's love on certain levels, and try to figure out how you can circumvent the limitations they faced. At the same time, you had to think of an interesting way to give them a challenge. One of the things difficult about this show was that there wasn't anywhere for their relationship to go. Almost by the end of the pilot they had this amazing, romantic love which we all dream of. So my challenge was this: how could she find a love like the one she had with Vincent that was actually possible? I came up with the idea of this disciple of his who had all of his qualities of character, but was 'a normal human being.' That's how the character of Michael came about.

"What we originally had in mind was that Catherine would start to fall for this kid. This was very exciting to the network and very exciting to us, because it was scary. It was a challenge to their relationship. Actually, there was no other character you could introduce that had a chance to vie for her heart against someone as amazing as Vincent. Elliot Burch was never really a believable romantic threat. Here was a character in Michael who had almost everything Vincent had, except obviously for the pain of his deep suffering background. The problem was that the more we worked on the story, the more we realized that the audience was absolutely going to rebel against the idea of her actually starting to fall for anyone else besides Vincent, so we kind of diluted the notion.

"We did get into some interesting areas. The scene a lot of people remember is the one in which Vincent grapples with the impossibility of her love and asks her if she wouldn't rather be with this guy. If so, he doesn't want to be in the way of her happiness. We got indirectly into something that was deeper. Even if she was never going to fall in love with this kid — and in the show he falls in love with her — the fact that Vincent can see that this man is in many ways worthy of her and the right person for her, it made it more difficult for him to possibly be standing in the way of her happiness. I think we were able to offer something pretty powerful in the episode, even though we weren't able to challenge them the way we originally wanted to."

Gus Trikonis muses, "That was interesting, because it was the reverse of 'God Bless the Child.' In the other one Vincent has the emotional upheaval, and here Catherine begins to have feelings about this young fellow who's come Above."

"The thinking behind it was trying to find Catherine a worthy suitor among the humans," explains Howard Gordon. "Who would it be but a man formed in Vincent's own image? But somehow this guy fell far short of Vincent and I don't think he was a serious enough threat for Catherine's affection. He came off as too much of a kid in that show to make that idea work properly. And, again, how many times can Vincent be jealous? And if he's gonna be jealous, it should be something that we also feel jealous about. The guy maybe should have been more physically beautiful, or at least more physically beautiful than Catherine. In the original concept, he was to be someone who really echoed Vincent's looks even, but in human form. Long blonde hair, tall…all these things, and he ended up being the guy who played the copy boy on *Slap Maxwell*. He's a good actor, but the casting really could have made a difference with that one."

Alex Gansa explains, "Here's an example of a story that was kicked around for a long time. Here was the reverse, interestingly enough, of the 'God Bless the Child' dynamic in which a younger person comes into Catherine's life and falls in love with her. You see, we were so limited in our possibilities. There wasn't a lot we could do with these two people, because they didn't interact on a daily basis in some society or in some community, where we could create drama. We were forced to do what I considered to be slightly artificial conflicts between Vincent and Catherine and this knight. Our focus was off. This was not a successful episode as far as I was concerned."

Episode 2.8
"Labyrinths"
Original Airdate: January 20, 1989
Written by Virginia Aldridge
Directed by Daniel Attias
Guest Starring: Philip Waller (Geoffrey), Armin Shimerman (Pascal), Laurel Moglen (Brooke), Ritch Brinkley (William), Ellen Geer (Mary), David Greenlee (Mouse), Jonathan Ward (Brian), Daniel Benzali (Edward), Jeff Maynard (Stevie)

A teenaged Dungeons and Dragons fan unlocks the secret of the underworld in "Labyrinths."

"To a certain extent, that show got screwed up along the way in its development," relates George R.R. Martin. "It should have been better. One of the things we ran into was strictly budgetary. In the original draft, the kid is much younger, like a 12-year old, who's really into D&D. When he finds this underground world, he really fantasizes that he's found a D&D world. Well, two things happened along the way. One, Ron felt that maybe the kid's psychotic to confuse reality with the D&D world, so that element got kind of soft-pedaled and removed, which I'm not sure I entirely agree with. I don't think it quite made the kid psychotic. It may have made him more of a kid who's a little disturbed, and I thought it was an interesting element. Then, of course, we ran up against the child labor laws, which no one had thought of until we got the first draft in and realized that the kid is in almost every scene. Well, you can only work with a minor child a certain number of hours in a day, and there was no way to make this a seven day shoot with all the scenes the kid was in, unless we went with an older kid. Instead of getting a 12-year old, we got like an 18-year old pretending to be a 15-year old. That changes things, too."

Says Alex Gansa, "I don't mean to short change any of these shows, but we're dealing with a guest star and there was very little emotional juice generated between our leads. It was a very interesting idea, but it was a struggle on staff as to how fantastical the boy's voyage into the underworld would be. Some of the staff argued that it should be very fantastical, because this boy has tremendous imagination, and other people argued that real fantasy would work against our own real world down there. So we ultimately chose to go the slightly more safe, more conventional route. He basically gets lost down there, is found and has to make a choice between the two worlds. It was a very hastily conceived episode, because we were scrambling to get to that point."

Episode 2.9
"Brothers"
Original Airdate: February 3, 1989
Written by George R.R. Martin
Directed by Beth Hillshafer
Guest Starring: David Greenlee (Mouse), Ritch Brinkley (William), Ellen Geer (Mary), Kevin Scannell (Charles), Bruce Abbott (Devin Wells), Don Stark (Eddie), Robert Britton (Bernie), Remy Ryan (Lauren)

Devin returns to the underworld, accompanied by a deformed man he has retrieved from a carnival freak show in "Brothers."

George Martin states, "I like 'Brothers' quite a lot. I think it's my favorite of my episodes. Of course, I got to bring back Devin, an interesting character with a lot of potential and a relationship with Vincent. 'Promises of Someday' addressed a lot of Father/Devin issues, but I think there were a lot of Devin/Vincent issues that were not addressed until 'Brothers.' I think it helps round out Vincent and explain some of the aspects of his personality. I think you can understand a character better if you understand his background. Of course, the other major feature of 'Brothers' was what we called the Dragon-Man. Sometimes for a writer working in television, there is a difficulty. You put things on the page and you never know how they're going to come out on the screen. Sometimes you lose a little — probably more often than not. It's never quite what you imagined it. But I also think that sometimes you gain, and 'Brothers' was one of those cases. Whatever I could have imagined was just so splendidly realized. We got very, very lucky with the casting and Rick Baker's make-up. It was an incredible travesty of justice when Rick failed to win an Emmy for that episode. It was really a disgrace. But I was very pleased with 'Brothers' all the way down the line. And it's interesting to compare the way the world Above and the world Below treats their misfits."

"Another George R.R. Martin masterpiece," proclaims Howard Gordon. "I really thought the Elephant Man echo was an appropriate one, and there were some very fine moments between them. When Vincent says, 'There are no freaks here,' that's a very poignant moment, and there's a scene between Vincent and Dragon-Man at the end that's really wonderful. And it's also Devin's redemption, which was well handled, and the two stories dovetailed nicely."

Alex Gansa concurs. "George just did an absolutely fantastic job," he says. "An episode that was filled with pathos, complexity and was by far his best. Although I wasn't a big fan of the Devin character, only because I thought there were too many parallels with somebody else we had on the show, Mitch Denton, but it was a great episode."

Episode 2.10
"A Gentle Rain"
Original Airdate: February 17, 1989
Written by Linda Campanelli & Shelly Moore
Directed by Gus Trikonis
Guest Starring: David Greenlee (Mouse), Ellen Geer (Mary), Ritch Brinkley (William), Chris Paul Davis (John), Piper Laurie (Mrs. Davis), Scott Jaeck (Kanin), Elayne Heilveil (Olivia)

Catherine discovers a hit and run drunk driver has been living Below for 18 years, and must bring him to justice in "A Gentle Rain."

"When we had gone in to pitch for the show," explains Linda Campanelli, "they asked us to come in with Catherine and Vincent stories. We came in with four Catherine and Vincent ideas and the premise of 'A Gentle Rain.' Naturally, they bought 'A Gentle Rain.'"

"The inspiration," adds Shelly Moore, "was a story in a magazine about someone who had not really done anything wrong in his life. But one mistake and it resulted in the death of an innocent victim. And I thought, 'What an awful thing to carry on your conscience. You screwed up one time, you didn't mean to do it, but for the victim's family you do need to pay or they feel as though they've been left out and can't have a sense of closure.' We took that in, and our initial idea had to do with a 17-year-old youth and a 7-Eleven robbery. He didn't mean to get involved with these people, he never would have tried a hold up again in his life and never had before, but someone behind the counter is now dead and he has to go to jail. Seventeen years later he's caught, despite the fact he's been a really great, great citizen trying to make up for that crime.

"Then, we decided that more people have been drunk behind the wheel of a car than have carried a gun into a 7-Eleven. To make it hit the heartstrings with more people across America, we called George and told him about our idea, and he agreed with us. When we made this change we really went to the other side, probably because Linda's the mother of two kids. When we turned in our first draft, we'd actually gone too far in that direction. The rest of the staff pulled it back in the other direction, and Linda and I feel that the final episode was pulled too far back and there wasn't enough sympathy for the mother. What came out on film seemed to be much more of a hysterical, out-of-control mother than someone who had suffered such a great loss. Her whole life had fallen apart and no one was there to help."

Campanelli interjects, "Other people on the staff thought she should be over it after six months, but our feeling was that it's something you never get over. We spoke to a woman who was a president of MADD, Mother's Against Drunk Driving, and she said that having someone say 'I'm sorry' is very important to these people. It's at least an acknowledgement of some kind."

Howard Gordon explains, "Lee Goldberg and Bill Rabkin came up with a story that didn't sell which was about a guard in a Nazi war camp. That idea was one we had been tampering with for a long time, but we felt there was something unredeemable about harboring someone who could be a Nazi war criminal. But someone who had been driving drunk when he was young, had killed someone and was incredibly repentant about it was. We established very early that they do not harbor criminals down there, although in a sense Father was a criminal and in a sense we had another one....actually we never did shoot it, but we had a story where Mary was involved in the student underground and indirectly involved in a bombing of a library that killed a security guard. That was an interesting story, and was going to be her backstory. Anyway, the kind of sanctuary the underworld provides was really the theme behind that one, and I think there were some really fine moments in it."

George R.R. Martin points out that, "This was the first script by Shelly Moore and Linda Campanelli, who were very valuable additions to our staff. They were really in love with the romantic aspects of our show which, oddly enough, despite the fact the show was considered a romance, was never the particular favorite of the other staff members. Ron Koslow always talked about the kind of mythic elements of the show. I was certainly in love with the science fiction/fantasy elements of the show; the boys liked the character drama. Until Linda and Shelly, we hadn't acquired people who wanted to do real Catherine and Vincent stories, as romantic as possible. They loved the romance of the show, and that was something I think we needed."

Gus Trikonis points out, "That's the show where there's a flashback of a little boy who gets killed by a car, and I put my son in that role. He desperately wanted to be in *Beauty and the Beast*, and that was his first time on film. We did it as a second unit shot after the picture had been finished. I went down with him that evening — it was all set up by the producers — and we did this piece of film on him where he yells and it's intercut with a guy banging and cutting away at the stones. I was driving home with my son and he said, 'I like this, dad.' I said, 'Oh shit, now I've got an actor on my hands.' It was a turning point in his life, because more and more he wants to be an actor."

Episode 2.11
"The Outsiders"
Original Airdate: February 24, 1989
Written by Michael Berlin & Eric Estrin
Directed by Thomas J. Wright
Guest Starring: David Greenlee (Mouse), Zachary Rosencrantz (Zach), Armin Shimerman (Pascal), Ellen Geer (Mary), Dennis Phun (Long), Anthony James (Micah), Jonathan Perpich (Randolph), Dan Bell (Dak), Chance Michael Corbitt (Zeke)

A group of individuals deemed psychotic decide to live Below in "The Outsiders."

"There was some feeling that the episodes were getting a little too internal," notes P.K. Simonds. "One of the things that excited viewers from the very beginning was the sense of jeopardy that was in many of the first season episodes. Part of the strength you had at that time was what had been becoming a formula: crusading Catherine gets herself into physical jeopardy and Vincent saves her dramatically. He destabilized them ...or taught them important lessons, such as how to walk with one leg. Anyway, the problem was that everyone, from the writers to the actors, was beginning to feel a little tired of that. This is the incredibly debilitating aspect of TV, in that you're asked to find something that works and repeat it.

"Even though the audience doesn't mind that, because they keep tuning in for more, the immense challenge you face is to try and make it seem like it's a little different. So the second season is when we potentially started to get away from that, and got into episodes that were different. Unfortunately, that coincided with a little bit of a ratings decline, and no one will ever know for sure whether this was because we departed from the formula, or whether in fact you've seen the fairy tale, at the end of the first season you saw some form of the kiss and that's the way it should have ended. 'The Outsiders' was our response to the network's want of physical jeopardy.

"What was interesting about it is the fact that, here you had one kind of community, and in other areas of the tunnels was another kind of community, which was an extremely opposite. We wanted to create characters who were utterly terrifying, and I think the way you do that is by creating characters who are devoid of any shred of humanity. In a way they're more terrifying, because our characters cannot even understand them."

"Up to this point," George R.R. Martin recalls, "we had been doing all character drama. I don't think Vincent had killed anyone or even beasted out in the previous second season episodes. Unfortunately, our ratings were going down, so 'The Outsiders' was our swing back towards action-destabilization...Vincent destabilized a lot of people in that episode, including the first woman he's ever destabilized. 'The Outsiders' began to pave the way to some of the later episodes in which he would confront his dark side. It of course also conveniently introduced Catherine Chandler's gun, which I would later pick up on in 'Invictus.'

"The other thing about 'The Outsiders' was an argument we had, which I lost. I would have liked to see the tunnel community do a little more to defend themselves there. I was always bothered by the fact that when faced with a threat, the tunnel community essentially let Vincent handle it. I would have liked to have seen more of Jamie and her crossbow, which is my favorite part in 'To Reign in Hell,' or the rallying of the people. At one point, we talked about the Outsiders storming the great hall, but people are there to defend it. The boys were doing some of the rewrite on that and Alex, in particular, was very opposed to that idea, hence his view prevailed. Interesting aspect about 'The Outsiders' is that at a key point there's a fight between Father and William, and if you look back at it afterwards, you realize that William is actually right. If they had listened to William, none of these bad things would have happened."

Says Howard Gordon, *"Beauty and the Beast* often treaded the line between camp and melodrama. This episode did yuk it up a bit. It was pretty violent and Vincent just kind of did a lot of blood-letting."

"This was a show that showed *Beauty and the Beast* at its very best, and at its very worst," notes Alex Gansa. "I think there were some wonderful things in that episode, mainly about what happens when a community is besieged and all the various rationalizations that go on in that community to try and reach out to people that are essentially the enemy. But, just as in 'No Way Down,' our villains for the most part never made it as real as it should have been. They never became real in my mind, and I think this was more true here than it was in 'No Way Down.' But nevertheless, these patently evil characters, basically fodder for Vincent and company, didn't quite sell as far as I was concerned. People were just up in arms over it, they just hated it. The fans were upset by the violence of the episode. It seemed gratuitous because our villains were not realized as characters. I loved when Catherine brought Father the gun and how the gun later came back to be used in an episode of the third season."

Episode 2.12
"Orphans"
Original Airdate: March 6, 1989
Written by Howard Gordon & Alex Gansa
Directed by Victor Lobl
Guest Starring: Philip Waller (Geoffrey), John McMartin (Charles Chandler), Abraham Alvarez (Dr. Cherian), Frederic Arnold (Jay Coolidge), Douglas Roberts (Mark Coolidge), Kate Williamson (Marilyn Campbell)

When Catherine's father dies, she retreats to the world Below to be with Vincent and not deal with her grief in "Orphans."

"'Orphans' was a bitch for Alex and me," admits Howard Gordon. "We really wrote it and rewrote it, rewrote it, rewrote it and rewrote it. When we filmed it, the director's cut was 20 minutes over, so there were huge sections that had to be excised from the final cut, which is unfortunate because I think they really did add depth to it. What was nice about the episode is that it explored the magical realism of *Beauty and the Beast*, where angels and ghosts exist, and when Catherine's father revealed himself, Alex and I actually fought very strongly for getting rid of the dream nature of the scene. The way it's framed now, she falls asleep while she's down Below and then her father appears to her. Basically, you see her fall asleep and wake up again. Alex and I really wanted to blur the possibility that maybe her father did come back at some level. We really didn't like the lateralization of that appearance, and thought it should be more serious. That's one of my big disappointments.

"It's kind of a slow moving episode. At the same time, I think it was effective. It really tended to be one of people's favorites, because it was very deeply a Vincent/Catherine story and it dealt with an issue that was on a lot of people's minds: why doesn't she just live with him down Below? Ultimately, what came out of it is because now is not the time for her to do it."

Alex Gansa points out that "Orphans" is "a very difficult episode for me to talk about, because this was a show that went through so much work. When you deal with somebody's father dying, everybody brings their own preconceptions, their own fears and their own passions to it. I think because of that very fact, dealing with that issue in any way basically evokes a lot of emotion on the part of people. They want it to be good and they want it to speak to their own experiences. It was by far the most difficult episode that Howard and I wrote. Although it turned out well, it was an example of an episode that I think was far better on the page than on the screen. That was largely because it was shot in a very lethargic way, and I think that Victor Lobl did some of our best episodes. In this particular instance, whether it was the script, the actors or Victor himself, or whatever combination of those factors, it created an extremely slow pace. I think that basically we spent too long on the moments, everything took too long and consequently we had to lose a lot of our favorite scenes from that show, which I think added a lot to the episode.

"For example, scenes that never got shot included Catherine seeing her father everywhere. She saw him in a cab at one time after he died, but there were moments in the underworld where she kept seeing him. He was this phantom in her consciousness, so that moment when he actually appears to her wearing the clown's nose became a much more powerful moment than it is now, just coming out of the blue. That's what we were really working towards. Also, the thing that I was most upset about was that after that sequence with her father, there was the implication that it was a dream. This all had to do with people wanting to make the moment accessible. They said, 'Okay, if she's dreaming, then I understand.' That wasn't the idea behind the scene. The idea was that she actually had a waking vision, a magical out-of-time vision of her father. However it happened, I think it was a magical experience that all of us have had in our lives at some level. Magical realism is what we were tying to go for, and that is what forces Catherine out into the world again. Not some dream that she had. Here was her father actually saying it was going to be okay, that she would get over this and everything would be okay. To me, that's far more powerful if it comes to her in a conscious way, whether it's a projection of her own ego or whatever, it's part of the healing process. It's not some dream she wakes up from in a sweat, which is a cliché. That was the one issue we fought over, and we won that one in the script stage, and they went ahead and did it anyway. I was always very upset with that. But I think we took a lot of chances with that episode.

"The very fact that we had her dad appear wearing a red clown's nose had everyone saying, 'How is this going to play? Are you serious? Are you joking?' Ultimately, it was a fairly powerful story, and Linda did an absolutely wonderful acting job in that episode. Also, the death of a parent brings your own mortality home, and this show got more response than any other that Howard and I wrote. There was a wonderful outpouring of response to the show. It was a good show, because it really dealt with our characters, which we strayed from. On the other hand, it was a very slow and somber episode, with a hopeful ending."

Comments George R.R. Martin, "A very moving episode, which I think should have been a two-parter, and at one point that possibility was discussed. There are really two things going on in there. One is Catherine dealing with the death of her father, but the other is that she comes Below to live with Vincent, and then decides to return to the world Above. That whole second beat, which is very important, is kind of crammed into the final act. I think the structure, and the boys would probably agree with me on this, would have been better if the first show had been about the death of

Charles Chandler, and at the end of that show, Catherine makes the decision to go Below and live in the tunnels. Then, the entire second show would be about consequences of that decision. But, for whatever reason, we didn't go in that direction."

Victor Lobl elaborates, "On the set, it was a quiet and reflective atmosphere during the shooting of this show, which was highly unusual for an episodic television set. It was very powerful, and we all kind of experienced it with Linda. I think it's more of a quality statement of where we all were with the show than anything else. My recollection is that that was the last episode that I felt was an attempt to deal with any real depth on a human, personal issue. From then on, I felt we were drifting.

"It felt as though there was a real hunt on for more aggressive storylines, with much more action. There was a growing restlessness with stories that allowed Catherine and Vincent to express their interior monologue. There was less and less of that, it seems to me, from that point forward. It felt like a transitional point in the series for us. It may also have been as a result of the intensity of that one show. Anything after that was just a little more open. That one was really so intense, internal and quiet, that everything else might have seemed more on the surface."

Episode 2.13
"Arabesque"
Original Airdate: March 13, 1989
Written by Virginia Aldridge
Directed by Thomas J. Wright
Guest Starring: Ellen Geer (Mary), Marcie Leeds (Samantha), Elyssa Davalos (Lisa Campbell), Christopher Neame (Collin), mark Neal (Young Vincent), Kelli Williams (Young Lisa), Preston Hanson (Frank), Marguerite Hickey (Beth), Michelle Costello (Jill), Linda Hoy (Marie)

"Arabesque" chronicles the return to the tunnel world of Lisa, Vincent's first love.

"A wonderful idea for an episode," smiles Alex Gansa, "and ultimately just poorly miscast. The woman was probably a very fine actress, but she was miscast and out of her depth on the show. I think ultimately the show, although it's not as successful as it might have been and, again, we shied away from a real confrontation between Vincent and Catherine which would've been nice, answered a lot of questions about Vincent. And about his extreme trepidation about getting involved with Catherine. It also spoke to his fear of women, what happened with Lisa, how he really did hurt her at some level. Again, there was a tremendous argument about how violent the previous episode was. As you might guess, Howard and I came down on the side of making it a serious, violent act. Let's really give this woman some scars. Unfortunately, that didn't happen. It got watered down a little bit, and became more of a scratch and Vincent fell unconscious as opposed to something really dramatic. I thought the show had one of our top 20 moments, when Catherine takes Vincent's hands into hers and says, 'these are my hands,' as she tried to tell him that it was okay. There were some powerful things in the show, but the casting didn't do it justice to the point that the episode suffered as a result."

"Disappointment," sighs Howard Gordon. "The idea was to have been Vincent's first experience with another woman, and exploring Vincent in the past and what his first experience with his own sexuality was. That's really what was behind that one, and I don't think it worked quite as well as it could have."

Episode 2.14
"When the Bluebird Sings"
Original Airdate: March 31, 1989
Written by Robert John Guttke and George R.R. Martin
Directed by Victor Lobl
Guest Starring: David Greenlee (Mouse), Carolyn Finney (Rita Escobar), Beah Richards (Narcissa), Terri Hanauer (Jenny Aronson), Franc Luz (Kristopher), Severn Darden (Mr. Smythe)

In "When the Bluebird Sings," Vincent and Catherine encounter Kristopher Gentian in the world Below, and the distinct possibility exists that he is actually a ghost.

"Another one of my favorites," says George R.R. Martin. "These are probably the reasons why I think the second season is my favorite of the three. 'Bluebird' was the kind of episode I thought we should be doing more of all along. It was a little lighter in tone and God knows, particularly in the second season, we needed some episodes that were a little lighter in tone.

"It was a spec script from Robert John Gutke, who is an artist living in Minneapolis with no prior writing credits. The only reason I even looked at it is because we have a mutual friend. Robert was just amazingly persistent. His early drafts were very amateurish and not even the right number of pages, something like a third as long as they needed to be. I kept sending it back to Robert, he kept rewriting it and sending it back to me. He did have a wonderful character in Kristopher Gentian, and the notion of a good idea. In the draft that we finally purchased from Robert, Kristopher is much more clearly a ghost. *Beauty and the Beast* always had this cardinal rule that Vincent and the underworld are our fantastic elements, which is why we didn't do stories that were occasionally pitched, like Vincent meets the Wolf Man. So it was necessary to take Robert's script and restructure it to walk a tightrope. Was Kristopher a ghost? Was he a hoax? The viewer is left in a position to make up his or her own mind about that. I have my own theory.

"Once again, Victor Lobl did a marvelous job directing, and our guest star was really splendid. I was very pleased with the way 'Bluebird' was done. I think the show would've been more successful ratings wise, though not necessarily artistically, had 'Bluebird' and shows like it been a larger portion of our mix."

For his part, Lobl notes, "We all had a really good time with that one. The sort of romantic atmosphere took over and everybody got swept up in it. As far as the ghost element, I don't think there was any moment when we thought that wasn't working for us; it felt very comfortable."

Howard Gordon considers this to be one of his favorite episodes. "I liked it because it really pushes the envelope as far as fantasy within the series," he notes. "George did the rewriting on it, and it was one of my favorites of George's. I just think it had the amalgamation of romance and fantasy that we should've done more episodes like, rather than devolving into 'Starsky and the Beast' or something. Generally, the addition of mythical creatures is a problem, but a ghost, for some reason, works. I think also we have established the magic of Vincent and the underworld enough that it wasn't hard to accept the possibility of a ghost."

Alex Gansa enthuses, "Great episode. A light fantasy kind of show we should've done more of. A whimsical show and one of our best. In my point of view, it was a ghost and I don't think we should shy away from that, just like we shouldn't shy away from Cathy's father appearing to her. I think these things are evocative, not troublesome. George handled it wonderfully, leaving it as ambiguous as he did. That's always really wonderful, and looking back on it I have to say that George did some amazing work. But George is someone with a tremendous amount of energy and passion for the show, that he was able to sustain longer than any of us. At that time, especially after our 'Orphans' ordeal, we were saying, 'Oh my god, can we write some real people now?' We were well into the second season and were getting damn tired, but George was able to maintain a real freshness, as evidenced by this particular show."

Episode 2.15
"The Watcher"
Original Airdate: April 7, 1989
Written by Shelly Moore & Linda Campanelli
Directed by Victor Lobl
Guest Starring: Carolyn Finney (Rita Escobar), Terri Hanauer (Jenny Aronson), John Michael Bolger (Detective Greg Hughs), David Neidorf (The Watcher), Joseph Carberry (Detective Greene)

Simply put, Catherine is stalked by a hidden foe in "the watcher."

Shelly Moore laughs, "After pitching many, many, many Catherine/Vincent stories and writing many, many outlines, all of which would ultimately be rejected and we would be sent back to the drawing board, there came a day when in 10 days they needed a script to be ready for shooting. We sat down and we actually started 'The Watcher' idea from the back end. We said, 'What would be the most terrifying situation to be in?', but we decided on that day that it would be to be trapped in the trunk of a car that was sinking in water and no one knew you were there. We decided that would be our last act, Vincent rescuing Catherine from a trunk that was sinking in a lake. Then we had to come up with a story to fill in the first three acts. We pitched the idea to George Martin, and he said, 'Wouldn't it be great if you went one step further and had Catherine actually die, and Vincent goes into death and brings her back?' We thought that was great; we'd actually kill Catherine and Vincent would go in and get her. Basically we just loved that fourth act so much, and the first three acts were just constructed to build up to that moment."

Says Linda Campanelli, "That was one of the most fun scripts I can remember writing. It just played on all of women's fears. It was fun to write someone alone in an apartment, scared, thinking that someone is coming to get her. There were, however, some decisions made in the editing that we don't quite understand. The Watcher is someone that was in the script. In the editing, every shot of the watcher was edited out and we don't quite agree with the decision, because it made people believe that there would be some large reveal at the end of the show, and there wasn't. It misled people, which wasn't our intention."

"A great genre piece in that a lot of the conventions of the suspense thriller were really well used," reflects Howard Gordon. "We had a moment where Vincent actually brings her back from the dead. Just the context and framing of the series allowed us to take sort of a conventional thriller and do something slightly different with it. Normally, the hero saves the heroine before it's too late, but in this case, he doesn't save her... she's dead. It really allowed their love to bring her back. I thought it was very effective, and better than a lot of movies I've seen with similar conventions. I really thought it was Shelly and Linda's best work."

George R.R. Martin agrees with this last point. "Probably the best episode they wrote for us," he says. "The ending of that episode, the anniversary, is Ron Koslow's. Shelly and Linda wanted to end it with Catherine saying, 'Hold me, hold me closer,' and they embrace on the balcony immediately after the rescue. Ron decided that the anniversary scene would add to it. They're both romantic themes, but different takes on romance. I know some people love the anniversary scene, and others feel it would be stronger if it ended with 'Hold me closer.' I probably would have ended it the way the girls wanted to end it, although the anniversary scene is nice the way it is.

"One of our more romantic episodes, with a lot of nice elements in it. Though 'Watcher' was a scary kind of guy, it was Steve Kurzfeld's decision in editing not to show his face. We actually filmed his face. Kurzfeld decided as he edited that it would be more spooky if we never saw the Watcher, and he became — just as people like that are in real life — this unseen presence. You don't know what he looks like, but he knows what you look like. I'd imagine it was a rather unpleasant surprise for the actor the night he tuned in to see his performance."

Victor Lobl points out that the episode was "technically very tough. A portion of it was very demanding schedule wise. We had a lot of night work and it made it physically very difficult. Linda was understandably nervous about the whole trunk in the water sequence, and that's something we were all very concerned about. The whole thing was a very tense situation. My biggest concern was that Linda would panic, and that is what would have created the problem. I did feel that 'The Watcher' was part of the drift I had mentioned. There were other shows around the time that I didn't shoot, which seemed to be heading toward gratuitous action that I wasn't comfortable with. I thought 'The Watcher' could be a rather interesting study of psychotic behavior, but the script never really did explore it on that level, and I was disappointed. That was the show that went through a lot of changes in postproduction. Any depth we would try to add was removed in an effort to beef up the action."

Episode 2.16
"A Distant Shore"
Original Airdate: April 14, 1989
Written by Marie Therese Squerciati
Directed by Michael Switzer
Guest Starring: David Greenlee (Mouse), Carolyn Finney (Rita Escobar), Andrew David Miller (P.A.), Alan Berger (Danny), Debra Engle (Gina Barrett), Andrew Bloch (Mel Rae), Sal Jenco (Richie)

Catherine goes to Los Angeles to gather information on a murder trial in "A Distant Shore."

George R.R. Martin says, "That was probably the weakest show of the second season. The story pitch to us was all about migrant families in California, and Cathy having to go out to the West Coast. There are illegal Mexicans coming in and they're being taken advantage of... it would have been a great episode of *Lou Grant*. The writer was very passionate about this. She'd done a lot of research and knew a lot about it, but Koslow didn't see what migrants had to do with the show. He did, however, like the element of Catherine and Vincent being separated, so essentially, we told this writer to take out all the parts of the show she felt passionate about and build it around the rest, and I think what came out was just a mess. But we needed a script at that point. I can never figure out, number one, what the hell the fuss is about. It's not like 'Nor Iron Bars a Cage' in which Cathy is about to take a job in a different city and will be gone forever. She going to California for three days, and Vincent is acting like the world is coming to an end. And the whole plot with the evil record producer and the bad guys, was real television — the kind of stuff we always try to avoid doing. The only twist this time was that Catherine had to handle it on her own, because Vincent can't come to her rescue. He can only pace around and say, 'I miss her.'

"Speaking of *Lou Grant*, one of the show's former actors, Robert Walden, wrote an unfilmed script for us. His episode was called 'Subterranean Homesick Blues,' which was about the 60s and focused on the character of Mary, and really told her backstory as a '60s radical and what had driven her underground, and the son she had left Above. It was a pure character piece and on the production schedule until our ratings decline, and we abruptly went on 'The Outsiders' /action tract. The episode was abandoned. When it became clear we had to choose something here and didn't have any action scripts to go, I tried to convince the powers that be to put 'A Distant Shore' aside and do 'Subterranean Homesick Blues.' I think that the decision was made to go with 'A Distant Shore,' because it was allegedly more romantic, and had these Catherine/Vincent fantasies, and the video they jacked in the middle of it, partly because the show came out short. The video was not in the script. We were looking at the footage, which was short and not real thrilling.

We had to do something to save the show. It had a little bit of action, but I think our series would've been better served if we had made 'Subterranean Homesick Blues.' It was character drama as opposed to writing, but I think it was a better piece of writing and a better dramatic episode than 'A Distant Shore.'"

Howard Gordon says," I think conceptually, it was interesting to separate them and test the strength of their bond over the span of a continent, but for some reason, it fell slightly flat. I think the concept was better than the execution."

Episode 2.17
"Trial"
Original Airdate: April 21, 1989
Written by P.K. Simonds, Jr.
Directed by Victor Lobl
Guest Starring: Armin Shimerman (Pascal), Bill Marcus (D.A. Moreno), Jayne Atkinson (Molly Nolan), Rosemary Dunsmore (Virginia Sheets), Amy Lynne (Amy Nolan), Scott Marlowe (Richard Nolan), Byron Morrow (Judge Swenson), Fritz Bronner (Rob Rand), Dale Swann (Peter Rundler)

"Trial" moves Catherine into the courtroom, where she tries to convict a child abuser who killed his offspring.

Victor Lobl says, "'Trial' was also not a terribly successful piece. It didn't really probe beyond that whole issue of child abuse and marital abuse. It seemed to me to be slightly exploitive of the Hedda Nausbaum case. Sometimes it's an interesting thing to mirror those events if you're able to get beneath the surface, but all we had going for us in the script was really the most obvious elements. I felt it was more of the same. Although there wasn't that much action, I felt it was exploitive. There was always this desperate attempt to get a bigger audience."

P.K. Simonds explains, "We wanted to do an episode that allowed Catherine to be a lawyer, but the problem is that there's no organic way to involve Vincent in the story. I think the show suffered from that, because his connection was extremely contrived emotionally. Interestingly, Linda Hamilton, for all of her complaints about what the show didn't have, didn't seem to really enjoy playing that stuff. Also, occasionally we would do very emotional episodes that were about other characters, but for Vincent and Catherine this particular episode didn't involve them as personally."

"Politically, we had a little problem with that one on staff," Howard Gordon admits, "in terms of the whole argument of exploitation. At that point, it was loosely based on the Hedda Nausbaum trial, and the comparisons were a little bit heavy-handed. What was good about the episode was seeing the character of Catherine in trial for the first time, really acting as a lawyer and defending her case. We had sort of seen her gathering evidence in a very investigative way, and never really saw her doing her thing. One of the flaws, in hindsight, is that it was a trial Joe was being slated for, and I think more could have been made about their relationship. That could have been deepened a little more, rather than some courtroom conventions, although Linda was great."

"Very good issue," offers Alex Gansa, "but ultimately we were not *LA Law* in this particular instance, although we tried to be. It was a show that clearly took the Hedda Nausbaum case that was going on in the newspapers, and really tried to extrapolate from that and tell a story about Cathy's convictions and Vincent's support of her. Ultimately, we had less of that and more of the courtroom stuff, which was upsetting in terms of storytelling. We wanted to focus on that other part and found it difficult to do, so what happened is that it turned into a more stale courtroom situation than what we were really shooting for. Also, we had lost some things during shooting which were very interesting in terms of Vincent's hearing and seeing these abused children everywhere. There's a wonderful surreal sequence that was written but was never realized, which added some complexity to the whole show. With that missing and the de-emphasis on Vincent and Catherine, I think it was a very ordinary show."

Episode 2.18
"A Kingdom By the Sea"
Original Airdate: April 28, 1989
Written by George R.R. Martin
Directed by Gus Trikonis
Guest Starring: Edward Albert (Elliot Burch), John Michael Bolger (Detective Greg Hughs), Dave Cadiente (Ramon), George Tovar (Pilot), R.G. Armstrong (Stanley Kazmarek), Ken Foree (Morley), Dean Norris (Biggs), Scott Wells (Tyler)

Elliot Burch has been marked for death and Catherine puts her life on the line to help him in "A Kingdom By the Sea."

"The return of Elliot Burch and again, I feel like I'm repeating myself here, I was pretty happy with all of the second season episodes," notes George R.R. Martin. "Some of the action sequences weren't as dramatic as I had written them, but that was primarily for budgetary reasons. This was the point, because of our declining ratings; we had swung back to more action-oriented kinds of situations, but with more interesting stuff than first season. In a lot of the first season shows, Catherine would be in trouble, Vincent would come, he'd tear four guys into bits and we'd have a little romantic scene at the end. The real turning point, as I've said, in the second season was 'The Outsiders.' In the history of the characters, after a period of peace in which their relationship was fairly stable and Vincent was almost returning to the old, pre-Catherine Vincent who didn't deal with the world Above very much and didn't have to kill. Suddenly, in 'The Outsiders,' that world forcibly imposed itself on them and Vincent once again gave into the dark side of his nature and had to take a life, albeit for a good cause.

"As we developed the action in the second half of the second season, that's what we explored once more. We didn't just use violence as act breaks or as episode breaks in the way we had first season, or as most television shows did. I think we actually tried to explore the consequences of violence. If you do kill that many people, what does it do to you? What does it mean to you? What does it say about the kind of person you are? In all of these episodes, we see Vincent wrestling with this, and that's certainly the case with 'Kingdom By the Sea.' I think one of my favorite scenes in that is after it's all over, Vincent has to return Below and wash the blood off of his hands, which is the first time we've seen him doing that.

"Also, the network was very leery about the whole idea of the kiss. There's a scene in 'Kingdom By the Sea' where Elliot kisses Catherine at the moment they think they are about to die, and she responds to the kiss to a certain extent. Vincent senses this through the empathic bond, and there's a scene later on when she goes Below and Vincent is wounded and kind of recovering from his brooding. He's really comparing himself to Elliot and saying that however much he may love this woman, he cannot be the kind of companion that Elliot would be. He brings up the kiss and Catherine tells him at the moment they kissed, she wished it had been him, and that's a very powerful scene I think. I would have liked to have ended that scene with Vincent very tentatively leaning over and kissing Catherine, but we were forbidden to by the network."

Director Gus Trikonis recalls working with guest star Edward Albert on a mini-series for Universal called *The Last Convertible*, and "in that Eddie Albert and I really hit if off, but he was an actor out of control. He would come on a set and chew the set up, emote to the point where his guts were hanging out. I said to him, 'This isn't acting, this is throwing up. You've got to have some control there.' So here we're doing a show again, and he has grown some and he's grown up. I said to him, 'Eddie, less is more here. Just simply do the work.' And it was a touching stone for him. He was able to allow himself to just be, without acting outwardly. He was simple, direct, and alive in a scene. I also felt that it was a turning point for him in the show, because he had a chance to under act and be a lot more powerful. I saw him growing continually from that point on."

"I thought it was exciting," states Howard Gordon. "In the ongoing Elliot Burch Saga, I thought it was a very effective story that combined action and really brought forth a lot of his backstory. George did his usual great job on it, and I really am very happy with what he did with Elliot Burch. I thought Elliot was kind of cartoony and very broad, but ultimately he really resonated over a whole range of emotional frequencies. I think the actor really came through, sometimes better than others, and he became a very rich character."

Adds Alex Gansa, "I think Elliot Burch really fulfilled some of the early promise that he had. He had some wonderful Marlon Brando stuff to do in this particular episode, which I thought was really nice."

Episode 2.19
"The Hollow Men"
Original Airdate: May 5, 1989
Written by P.K. Simonds, Jr.
Directed by Victor Lobl
Guest Starring: David Greenlee (Mouse), Bill Marcus (D.A. Moreno), Cindy Lou Adkins (Karen Alexander), Rhonda Aldrich (Phoebe), Brian Bloom (Cameron Benson), John Diehl (Vernon), Apollo Dukakis (Judge Haignor), Hal England (Mr. Benson), John Garwood (Mr. Hallowell), Francois Giroday (Warren Brancton), Amanda Goodwin (Wendy)

Catherine and Vincent go up against a pair of rich teenagers who kill for the sheer pleasure of doing it.

"This is right up there with the voodoo show as our nadir," Alex Gansa moans. "I argued vehemently for two seasons against the idea of doing a thrill-kill story. Every other show on television was doing it. Turn to *Matlock*, *Miami Vice*, *Spenser: For Hire*…everywhere you turned, there were two rich college guys pumping iron and wielding knives and listening to Beethoven. Anyway, our dearth of stories forced us to do this show."

Howard Gordon quickly agrees. "That may be the very worst episode of *Beauty and the Beast* ever produced," he laughs. "It was one of those things that sort of occurred. It's something we had seen before everywhere. A convention, and we didn't do much new with it."

"I don't think anyone was sentimentally attached to the episode," says P.K. Simonds, one of numerous writers who took a crack at this particular script. "We found some stuff in the episode that was good. A little bit of exploration of Vincent's dark side, the fact that he understood something in these kids. Just from looking in their eyes he knew more about them than anyone else. He sensed that he was the only one who could stop it, because of this sort of interesting dilemma of not being able to come forward, which obviously gave him a greater sense of responsibility. Interesting stuff, but, personally, I don't like writing psychotic or neurotic characters."

Notes George R.R. Martin, "The script kept being considered and rejected. Sometimes they were killing homeless people; sometimes they were killing prostitutes or members of the underground. It kept varying, but never successfully. But towards the end of the second season, we hit a script crunch — as they're sometimes optimistically called — and we looked to the scripts we rejected, and pulled that one. P.K. Simonds rewrote it, reconceived certain elements and made it better than most of the early versions, although it still was not a great script."

"I actually got chills a couple of times," relates Victor Lobl, "when I felt we got really close to sensing what those moments of death are like in reality. I thought the script ultimately backed off in the end when it became a sort of fantastical ending. I think we all felt let down by that. Very often the script conceptually offered challenging ideas and then they didn't really fulfill them. The process of working on the set, actually trying to bring this stuff to fruition would give us the sense that we were working the problems through up to a point. So, there was a certain amount of gratification.

"I think starting with 'The Watcher,' Linda Hamilton, particularly, became extremely vocal about her displeasure with the scripts and the way they were heading. And Ron Perlman joined in shortly thereafter. She constantly pushed for better scripts, trying to fulfill an idea and I think she grew frustrated by that. The ironic thing is that they pushed for better scripts, but couldn't offer concrete examples of what they had in mind."

ALTHOUGH NO ONE REALIZED IT AT THE TIME, AS SEASON TWO WAS
WINDING DOWN SO WAS LINDA HAMILTON'S TIME WITH THE SERIES.
(PHOTO: CBS).

Episode 2.20
"What Rough Beast"
Original Airdate: May 12, 1989
Written by Howard Gordon & Alex Gansa
Directed by Michael Switzer

Episode 2.21
"Ceremony of Innocence"
Original Airdate: May 19, 1989
Written by George R.R. Martin
Directed by Gus Trikonis

Episode 2.22
"The Rest is Silence"
Original Airdate: May 26, 1989
Written by Ron Koslow
Directed by Victor Lobl
Guest Starring: Edward Albert (Elliot Burch), Tony Jay (Paracelsus), Gary Hudson (Gus), Don Maxwell (Roger), Jim Meltzer (Steven Bass), Dan Shor (Bernie Spirko), David Greenlee (Mouse), Armin Shimerman (Pascal), Ritch Brinkley (William), Irina Irvine (Jamie), Beah Richards (Narcissa)

The second season concluded with the so-called *Beauty and the Beast* Trilogy (episode titles "What Rough Beast," "Ceremony of Innocent" and "The Rest is Silence"), which explored Vincent's dark nature unlike any previous episode had done. Paracelsus devises a plan to drive Vincent to the point of madness when he will give in to his darker nature. As a result, this trilogy gave the series an undeniably harder edge than had been seen before.

"Part of that had to do with the network directive," explains Howard Gordon. "If we wanted to stay on, we had to get the edge back, and one of the ways we thought of doing it organically was to explore Vincent's character."

Elaborates George R.R. Martin, "Essentially, Howard, Alex and I had plotted the first part of that trilogy together. Then, they did 'What Rough Beast' and I wrote 'Ceremony of Innocence' and Ron Koslow finished the trilogy with 'The Rest is Silence.' He wasn't really part of the plotting, and kind of picked up the ball from the rest of us. I was very proud of the trilogy, and I think it's as good as anything we did. The three episodes were very different, but built the way we wanted them and there was some wild stuff in there. It really did take us to a whole new place with the character; a place we hadn't seen Vincent before. I think Roy Dotrice did some of his best work. Not only did he play Father, but he played Paracelsus as Father."

"I would say the only bad thing about the trilogy was losing Paracelsus. I loved the character. There were elements connected with our show in the studio and the network…essentially in some sense there was a realistic camp and a fantasy camp. And Paracelsus and the world Below were definitely in the fantasy camp. There were those elements who felt the show would be more successful if it was more of a cop show, more of the *Hulk*, more reality based and less fantasy-oriented. Obviously, I was not in that camp, and Paracelsus was definitely thought of as the wilder, fantasy side of our show."

Alex Gansa adds, "You can put names on the episodes but in truth this was a real collaboration on the staff and ultimately I think it became the most fun time on the staff that any of us had had, and we really needed it at that point to inject each other with some adrenaline and enthusiasm. I personally think those last three shows are fantastic. They're admittedly dark, and full of *sturm und drang,* and operatic in a way, but I think taken as a whole, it's stuff you don't see on television very often. I think it's very interesting the way the shows built.

"We started with what we hoped would be very conventional storytelling. We started with a reporter story, Vincent being exposed, Paracelsus playing his tricky games and ultimately tried to build a credible foundation for Vincent's demise. Here was someone from the outside world affecting Vincent at such a deep level that he was already beginning to feel unstable. I remember the last shot of that show, moving in on Vincent's eyes, was just fantastic. Paracelsus, a character I personally gave birth to, was wonderful as was Elliot Burch. If *Beauty and the Beast* was supposed to tell stories that no other show could do, these three episodes proved it. They were so full of energy and pace, and largely what we had been missing through the whole season. The moment when Vincent imbeds his claws in who he thinks is Father…can you imagine a wilder moment on television? And the cliffhanging moment of the trilogy, when it sounds like he's attacking Catherine? Just amazing.

"'The Rest is Silence' was the dénouement of the story. The first two shows really de-escalated into a very psychological show, the last one. The pace was slower and we were coming down from that wave of violence. Interestingly enough, at the same time Vincent was getting more and more bestial. I think the currents and levels of storytelling, being told all throughout those three episodes, represented the staff at its finest. But I guarantee you that there are people who would 100% disagree with it. Not only on staff, but in the general public. We expected some conflict, but got a much more positive response. Some fans went crazy. They said, 'Vincent wouldn't feel these things, he's too noble'…Give me a break. He's a beast, for God's sake."

Says Howard Gordon, "Everything congealed for us, and that was a big turning point in the series. I also got a lot of shit from the fans on that one. People didn't want to see Vincent's dark side, and the whole thing was the exploration of what it meant to be Vincent, what exactly was he, what forces are working on him. Yes, it really evolved into this whole Luke Skywalker/Darth Vader battle for his soul, but I thought it was actually a very effective trilogy that worked to my taste. Even though we offended some, I think many people really supported the trilogy.

"A lot of people were very upset, as I recall. I guess there were different sections of fandom. Some were really into Vincent's quiet side and meditative side and his Christ-like side. When you show this kind of demi-god in compromised and violent terms, people really got offended...some people got offended. But I'm proud of what we accomplished."

Tony Jay, who concluded his portrayal of Paracelsus in the trilogy, notes, "I particularly like that small scene with the reporter where he dies a terrible death at Paracelsus' blade. It was totally unexpected, I thought, but it all made sense. The script was beautifully thought-out, and it was nice to have Paracelsus in everyday clothes for a change. If Paracelsus is brought back some day, and it is a big if, I would like to see him as the alter ego of Vincent; symbolizing what Vincent could've become had it not been for the tender graces of his other side and the effect that Cathy and Father have had on him."

"Ceremony of Innocence" director Gus Trikonis says, "Roy was terrific in a scene where he is supposed to really be Paracelsus. I thought it was a hell of a good episode and Tony Jay was absolutely terrific. It also provided a necessary exploration of Vincent's darker side."

Victor Lobl, who directed "The Rest is Silence," points out, "That actually was gratifying, because there was a feeling of closure to that, even though it was leaving the door open as a cliffhanger. There was a tremendous amount of dialogue in terms of which way to go, and that script was hammered out over a long period of time, worked and reworked. It was such a delicate issue to figure out how we were going to set up the following season, which was a question mark in itself. We were kind of finding a way to close the season strongly enough that we could live with it if that's where we were going to end, and at the same time whetting people's appetites for an interesting continuation. Nobody actually knew where we were going to go after that. There were some ideas, but nothing concrete."

And so, the trilogy ended on a cliffhanger, with Catherine's life possibly in danger at Vincent's hands. It was certainly an auspicious way to conclude the season, yet the general consensus on staff was that the year had not been as successful as season one.

Victor Lobl, who directed the season finales of years one and two, comments, "Whereas the end of the first season was on a tremendous high because we were absolutely certain we were going to be back, the end of the second year was more of a relief that the season was over and we could all take a rest. We were all very tired from a long season under difficult working conditions. In addition, there was clearly the sense that it was a divergence in opinion regarding the direction the scripts should go. It was a little sense of unrest in terms of whether or not the show would continue, because it might fall apart creatively or whether the show had in fact already taken the creative turn in a direction that was about to bring about its own demise.

"Also, we were all very much a family, and there was a certain kind of pride that is rare on any television set that I've been on. There was a sense of, 'Uh-oh, the stuff that happened on other sets is beginning to happen here.' It wasn't really out of control, but it was surprising to find that it was happening at all, because we were so tightly knit and so excited about what we were doing. They were just little seeds of discontent and unrest that were familiar to us all, and I don't think anybody knew what to expect the next season, particularly if the network continued to push us in an action direction that would make us look like other shows. The truth is that even though I felt it did become too action-oriented, there still were ingredients that set us apart radically from almost every other show."

"We made some large mistakes in the second season," muses Alex Gansa. "You look back and say we made a mistake, but at the time we made what we obviously thought was the best choice; hindsight is always a lot clearer. We were all excited in the second season, because we basically had free reign and thought we would tell stories we really wanted to tell. Our first mistake was not starting with an episode that followed 'A Happy Life,' because that show represented such a turning point in their relationship, and we needed a show that spoke to that fundamental change. What we did instead was just proceed as though nothing had happened.

"The nature of television is that by the time you see yourself in a rut it's too late. The metaphor is that you're an oceangoing vessel. You can't make a sharp left turn or sharp right turn, because you have so much momentum going. At the beginning of the season, we were just so dark and telling the small stories, that by the time we turned the ship, we left a long line of the sort of sentimental and sad and dark stories in the wake. That's why in the first part of the season there's one kind of story, and in the second part, there's another."

Notes Howard Gordon, "In hindsight, we should have gone back to 'A Happy Life,' and dealt with that moment when they sort of kissed. What happened when we started the second season was that a familiarity and a certain ease had developed between Ron and Linda off camera and during the summer. So I don't think we dealt with the ramifications of the end of the first season properly, and suddenly they had settled again into this familiarity and sameness that didn't really allow them to grow.

"At the same time, I think we liked a lot of the stories of the second season. No matter how good the vehicle was, it was always about their love by taking away some of the tension between them, which we did by having them be so familiar, I think something was missing. The thing that people wanted to see was this impossible love.

"Generally speaking, I think we were trying to really get into Vincent's beast aspect and discovering what it meant. To have fangs and claws. That means something. The way he looks has got to stand for something, yet we were really kind of ignoring that. He was incredibly well spoken, and his bestial side had remained unexplored. The nature of that was something we really wanted to flesh out and explore, and one of the ways we did that was to ask what did it mean, what would it mean, and what could it mean? We really explored the arch types of the beast and what it meant. Did it mean logical behavior? Instinctual behavior? How do you distinguish between bestiality and human anger? Do you just give Vincent a temper? Those moments were born out of an exploration of that part of his nature."

Director Gus Trikonis is pleased with the second season in that it taught him a great deal about his craft by allowing him to work with a crew that had largely come from motion pictures. "Their whole attitude was 'feature quality work,'" he muses. "The whole unit kept growing from one episode to the next, and I was rejuvenating myself. I kept opening myself up creatively to the point where we kept taking more chances with angle, light and performance. At the end of the season, after all my years in the business, I felt as though I learned more than all the other years combined. When the third season started, I was just ready to tear that film apart.

"And I thought that the second season worked overall. I felt they had to make the transition they made in order to keep it moving, because it did at some point become redundant between she and he. You know the relationship can't last on that level. Things change, we change. It had to go somewhere, it couldn't stay the same. I thought it had really reached a peak by the end of the second season."

"I thought the second season had some of the highest highs and some of the lowest lows," admits P.K. Simonds. "There were a couple of episodes that were really fantastic, but because we took a lot of chances, the failures seemed to be somewhat more conspicuous."

George R.R. Martin feels that season two was the show's best. "Not to say it was perfect," he clarifies, "and I could pick up mistakes in shows in all three seasons, if I wanted to. But I think we did some of our best work during the second year. If you look at all 22 shows, there's a tremendous range there; a tremendous diversity of shows. Unfortunately, they were mixed up. The first half of the second season was all character pieces, relatively slow drama, slowly paced. The second half was the more action oriented shows. If we had mixed it up, and had one one week and the other the next week, I think we would've had a show where anything could happen; you wouldn't know what you're going to get from week to week. It could be a serious dramatic show, it could be action oriented, it could be dark in tone, it could be light."

LINDA HAMILTON'S DEPARTURE IN THE THIRD SEASON MEANT A
COMPLETE REIMAGINING OF THE SERIES. (PHOTO: CBS).

SEASON THREE

For all intents and purposes, *Beauty and the Beast* was going to be cancelled at the conclusion of its second year, which was a bit of a shock to Ron Perlman, among others.

"We sat in the office of one of the CBS executives two weeks before the fall schedule was announced and were told that the network loved the trilogy we had shot to end the season so much that they wanted to use the second part of the trilogy as a cliffhanger to end the season and then use the final part to open the next season," Perlman told *The Orange County Register* in July 1989. "Doesn't that sound like a hint that they planned to put us on the fall schedule? Besides that, we had been kicking NBC's butt regularly in our time slot, the Viewers for Quality Television had voted us the best show on television, and we knew how loyal our fans were. We figured that CBS wouldn't dare cancel us. I was so confident, I left for Amsterdam on a vacation. And that's where I got the news."

Outcry from fandom actually convinced the network to change its corporate mind, though the show would only be renewed for 12 episodes and would likely be a mid-season replacement series. Additional bad news came from the fact that Linda Hamilton had every intention of leaving due to her pregnancy and the decision-makers became convinced that the audience was more interested in action than romance.

"I feel it's one of the better-done shows that we have," said CBS' then president Kim LeMasters. "I think that the problem ended up being that it just began to implode on itself. We had to loosen it up. No pun intended, if it were a roaring success, maybe we wouldn't. But the facts are we had an audience decline that made it unacceptable. If it's offended our audience, I'm truly sorry, but it wasn't large enough in the first place to warrant its stay."

LeMasters noted that Hamilton would be in the two-hour premiere. Koslow added that "Vincent will enter a new phase of his life, and there's a new quest on the horizon. The romantic tone of the show won't be changed, but there will be a much greater scope."

As initially conceived, the third-year *Beauty and The Beast* would have begun with the second trilogy that wrapped up elements left over from year two. Interestingly, the shows would've included the late Paracelsus.

"One of the phantom third season episodes would have involved Paracelsus, but he would still be dead," explains George R.R. Martin. "When we did the second season trilogy, we thought we were going to have a full third season of 22 shows starting in the fall. The question was, 'How would the trilogy have concluded?' It was left as a cliffhanger. The way we were going to come out of it the following September was with another trilogy called 'The Land of the Dead Trilogy.' Basically what Catherine finds in the cavern, and the reason she screams in 'The Rest is Silence,' is that she found Vincent and he's seemingly dead. In the following shows, he is sealed in the catacombs, Catherine grieves and goes on with her life and the underworld has to deal with this loss.

"As we're dramatizing that, we're also cutting to Vincent in the Land of the Dead, where he's dealing with all the people that he's killed through the years. Characters from previous shows, thugs, villains, and so forth, with Paracelsus, of course, presiding over them. At the end of this, his love for Catherine would bid Vincent to return to life. Once again our intent was to walk a tightrope. Was Vincent really dead and in the Land of the Dead? Or was he in some strange catatonic state that resembles death, in which he had this wild dream? That would never have been resolved, but ultimately Vincent would've woken up from his 'death,' and they would have had this experience."

This idea was abandoned when, as noted previously, Linda Hamilton announced that she was pregnant and would be leaving the series to pursue a "career" in motherhood.

To deal with the reduced episode order of year three, the staff came up with a 10 episode" arc" in which Catherine, who is carrying Vincent's child, is kidnapped by a villain named Gabriel. He keeps her alive long enough to have the child and then kills her. The remainder of the storyline has Vincent seeking his son and waiting to unleash his vengeance against Gabriel. Aiding him in this matter is an investigator named Diana Bennett, who finds out the truth about him, Catherine and the underground.

"When we returned for the third season," Martin details, "we knew Linda was leaving and had several decisions to make. Should we introduce a new female lead? Well, obviously, you do have to introduce a new female lead. Do you recast Catherine, or do you somehow get rid of the character and introduce a new one? If you go the route of getting rid of Catherine, do you kidnap her, kill her or have her take a job in another city? That's what we discussed for some time.

"If we just had Catherine kidnapped, that would have left the door open for her return, yes, but it really would have put the show on a permanent straitjacket. Vincent could never have forgotten about her. We would never be able to do a third-party show where he helps Rolley, Dragon Man or someone like that. We would never have been able to do a whimsical show, because Catherine was missing. So, every week, Vincent would hunt for Catherine, which was really not sustainable. A job in another city doesn't really make sense after all they've been through. So, the alternatives got discarded pretty quickly. That left us with the alternative of recasting or killing her and introducing someone else. Obviously you know the decision we made. We didn't think that recasting would work. It was probably the safest choice, although it's very seldom been done successfully in primetime television. We chose the alternative that we thought gave us the most dramatic possibilities."

On Catherine's death, Howard Gordon adds, "We just felt that many great love stories do end in death. Her moving away would be kind of anti-climatic, and we felt that the idea of recasting wouldn't have worked. Perhaps it would have in hindsight. That's what Monday morning quarterbacks seem to be saying. But we felt that her death was the only exit grand enough for the character. We went back and forth and argued for weeks and weeks about it, and obviously came to a decision and stuck with it.

"By killing Catherine the way we did, part of it was that Vincent would have an adversary worthy of his vanquishing. There is this kind of convention that when Charles Bronson's adversary rapes and murders his wife and daughter, it kind of tweaks up the revenge aspect. Perhaps we should have been less violent, but Gabriel was so insidious, and this was one way to reflect the depth of his insidiousness.

"We discussed the thought that Vincent couldn't have a love interest right away. It would have to be something that developed over the course of time, if at all. It was really a test period. We did the arc to really redefine how we would have told stories in Linda's absence. We probably would've done more like *Wiseguy* and told broader, more epic stories over two or three episodes at a time. A lot of it was the testing ground, and a lot would evolve depending on how Diana and Vincent worked together on screen. One of the best ways we thought to introduce a new character was through the case, and a character who ultimately would help Vincent find Catherine's killer. We also tried to explore a character who was different from Catherine."

"Diana had to be different; otherwise you just got a second-rate Catherine," interjects George R.R. Martin. "We wanted a whole different dynamic, and a relationship with Vincent that would not duplicate Catherine's by any means, but would take us to new places and give us new possibilities we had not seen before. We were extraordinarily fortunate in our casting. I think Jo Anderson was just sensational and the character was really terrific."

Early on, Ron Perlman remained enthusiastic about the new direction. "Basically what we've done is risen to the potential that the original concept provided us," he said. "In the middle of the second season, I thought that doing little one-hour episodes was missing the boat. I think it's time for *Beauty and the Beast* to assume the mantle it has danced around, which is to do things like theater, because you have this character, neither man or animal, who could be anything."

Episodes 3.1 & 3.2
"Though Lovers Be Lost"
Original Airdate: December 12, 1989
Written by Ron Koslow, Alex Gansa & Howard Gordon
Directed by Victor Lobl
New Regular Cast Member: Jo Anderson (Diana Bennett)
Guest Starring: Armin Shimerman (Pascal), Edward Albert (Elliot Burch), Bill Marcus (D.A. Moreno), David Greenlee (Mouse), Stephen McHattie (Gabriel)

The first episode of the season, "Though Lovers Be Lost," begins with Vincent near death, Catherine's love (and, yes, their relationship is finally consummated) reviving him and then the plot line unfolding as described above.

"I thought the episode was good, but it could have been great," says Howard Gordon. "What I liked about it was the introduction of Gabriel. Stephen McHattie is a great actor. He looks like he can rip out your throat with his teeth. At some level, you have to pay respect to the conventions of villainy. How evil can you get? One of my favorite scenes in the two-hour movie was Gabriel talking to the doctor, explaining how he killed his own father...really sick stuff. It fleshed a little bit of his character out."

Alex Gansa sadly notes, "A lot of the magic left the show, and I think 'Though Lovers Be Lost' was responsible. We did have to change the show. The new order from the network was action/adventure, no more romance and fantasy. We had to keep this thing as hard-driving as we possibly could. As a staff, that wasn't our strength. We weren't great action plotters. We were much better off on the romantic end of things.

"There were other things we could've done. All of us were *so* angry at Linda at the time, and have since come to understand that she was in a situation where she was going to have a baby. We should've said, 'Go out and enjoy your life.' Who are we to try and hold her back, but, at the time, we were upset. We knew that it probably signaled the death of the show, that it wasn't likely to go on for as many years as we would want. It was the death knell, and I think ultimately that's the reason we treated Catherine so miserably in the first two-hour show. We just did not treat the character with much love or affection at all. Those were some of the seeds of destruction. I also think we were tired, nobody knew if the show was coming back and when we found out it was, we had to change it.

IN SEASON THREE, JO ANDERSON JOINED THE SHOW AS PROFILER DIANA
BENNETT WHO PUTS TOGETHER THE PIECES OF THE LATE CATHERINE
CHANDLER'S PRIVATE LIFE (PHOTO: CBS).

"On the positive side, the episode certainly had some movement to it, there's no doubt about it. Vincent unsuccessfully trying to reach her was something we'd never done before. The introduction of Gabriel, who was great. Ultimately, I think it was a pretty powerful two hours of television. Not the *Beauty and the Beast* that people have come to expect, but it certainly launched us on our new road. I think it also showed that this was a series that was not going to get any more attention than it already had. We couldn't have had more promotion, publicity or hoopla for killing off a major character, and we still only did a 21 or 22 share. I think that everybody found from this experience that this was a very special show that was not going to attract a huge audience. It was a cult kind of show, and I think this demonstrated it once and for all. Even though we tried to take it out of that cult, even though we tried to make it more accessible, even though we tried to give people a villain they could hate, even though we gave Vincent a mission in the true sense of the word — in this case, a child to find — this was a show that was not going to have a mass following. Again, that depressed the hell out of all of us."

"There was actually strong network opposition to the whole idea of a child," states George R.R. Martin. "Believe it or not, one major network executive wrote a very strong memo to Kim LeMasters and referred to it as bestiality, which just grates on my mind. It's like you spend two seasons doing a show about the romance between a white man and a black woman or something, you finally get to the point where they're going to get together and you get a memo saying, 'They can't be together, that would be an interracial consummation.' Didn't anybody pay attention? The whole theme of our show for two seasons was that appearances don't matter, love transcends all. This one network exec just didn't get it, and found the whole concept of Vincent and Catherine being together disgusting. He compared it to a dog! Ron Perlman, even in Rick Baker's makeup, is not the same thing as a pony. This is a person, maybe he's a deformed person, but it's not taking sexual advantage of an animal. It's nuts. But I don't want to give the impression that this was the network position. This was the position of one executive, who lost."

Director Victor Lobl says, "We were dealing with the realities of television. At the beginning, we all said, 'How can we continue to shoot *Beauty and the Beast* without Beauty?' but when you get into it and start developing the storyline and the reality takes over, if you buy into it.

"I liked the new character, actually. I thought Diana was an interesting, different female lead. Also, the epic size of the story on top of what was already rather grand was very exciting to deal with. The action in 'Though Lovers Be Lost' was, for me, not offensive. I found that within the story it seemed purposeful and it worked. My problems were that it continued on and seem to escalate through the season. But, actually, that two-hour episode worked very well. It also allowed us to take bigger steps than we would have on the seven-day schedule we'd normally have. There was a freshness to it as well, and because it was the beginning of the season, everyone's energy level was very high. It seemed like a new and interesting challenge, and nobody knew where it was going. We didn't know what was going to happen."

Episode 3.3
"Walk Slowly"
Original Airdate: December 13, 1989
Written by Shelly Moore & Linda Campanelli
Directed by Gus Trikonis
Guest Starring: Edward Albert (Elliot Burch), Teri Hanauer (Jenny Arsonson), Lew Horn (Dr Marks), Lewis Smith (Mark), Stephen McHattie (Gabriel)

"Walk Slowly" has Vincent returning Catherine's body to her apartment, with an investigation into her death ensuing. This episode introduced Diana Bennett (think Clarice Starling from *Silence of the Lambs*) as the person searching for her killer.

Notes Shelly Moore, "Linda and I perceived Diana Bennett as a much warmer, family oriented and family-based person. We thought that Catherine during the first two seasons became more and more estranged from friends and family. After her father died, she was basically left with her adopted family from the tunnel community."

Linda Campanelli adds, "We wanted to have someone very different from Catherine, and we wanted her to be a part of a big family and close to that family. She was to be excellent in her work, very confident about herself, but she was someone who had trouble making relationships work. The Diana Bennett that ultimately came out of 'Walk Slowly' wasn't that character. I think that was a disappointment, because I would have liked watching our concept more, but we couldn't convince anyone else."

"We've gotten wonderful feedback from the fans," points out Moore. "Linda and I didn't come away absolutely excited about the episode, but the fans seem to love it. In all fairness, Alex and Howard also put a lot of work into that effort, and Ron wrote Vincent's voiceover eulogy."

Of this show, George R.R. Martin says," A very moving episode. Linda and Shelly did a terrific job for us. Ron Koslow contributed the eulogy that Vincent reads as Catherine is being buried, and it was enormously moving."

Alex Gansa notes, "Diana Bennett was good, although there were was no chemistry between Vincent and her at all, and that was a major problem. I think that Linda Hamilton, as an actress, was a more giving actress. She just gave everything to Ron Perlman when they were together on screen, because

Vincent and his mask had to be reactive. He needed the person he was on screen with to really give him stuff to play off of. Jo Anderson is a good actress, but she just wasn't a real giving actress, so the scenes between them weren't at the same level of intensity that we were used to with Vincent. But this was an episode that really worked. We needed an episode of mourning for Vincent."

THE BOND BETWEEN VINCENT AND DIANA BEGAN AS ONE OF RESPECT AND EVENTUAL FRIENDSHIP. WHETHER OR NOT IT COULD HAVE DEEPENED, NO ONE COULD BE SURE. (PHOTO: CBS).

Howard Gordon adds, "'Walk Slowly' presented us with the question of what the proper mourning time is for this relationship. It also begs the question of Diana in the beginning; we wanted to intimate that this was a possible relationship. If *Beauty and the Beast* was going to survive, there had to be a new beauty. This was a testing ground to see whether or not Jo Anderson was going to work, and whether or not there would be that kind of possibility or chemistry.

"The creation of her character was a coupe, I think. How it would have worked, I don't know, but conceptually it was a great character, the idea of a woman being hired, who is the best; a woman who is very different from Catherine, but who has the same kind of intensity, sensitivity and goodness that she had. And she is someone who could pick up on the pieces of the details and the whispers of this creature's existence in this woman's life. Whether or not it worked on screen between them, I'm not sure. We never really got a chance to test it."

Says Gus Trikonis, "It's a show about Vincent mourning Catherine's death. I thought Perlman was brilliant in the scene where he brought her body back to her apartment. The whole montage of him sitting there and the changes going on around him worked out great. Daylight is showing up, birds are singing and he has to leave her body for the last time. Even though she was gone, Catherine's presence pervaded the whole third season, and Ron Perlman had a lot to do with that, because he kept fighting over the fact that you don't let something like that go so easily. Through each show there was always something there, because it's something that's just not forgotten. 'Walk Slowly' was a totally draining show for Ron. I feel he did some of his best work for us in that show. You know, when he did that scene with Father, he resisted it. He couldn't get a handle on it. He couldn't understand what the scene was about. Roy and I sat and talked it through with him.

"One of the great scenes in that show, I felt, was the one where he goes to Father and Father says, 'Let her death wash over you; don't resist it.' I just lost my mother, and what kept coming back to me was that scene and how important it was and how it affected me, even though we shot it a year before. It was very helpful to me, because that's exactly what I had to do with my mother."

Episode 3.4
"Nevermore"
Original Airdate: December 20, 1989
Written by P.K. Simonds, Jr.
Directed by Victor Lobl
Guest Starring: Edward Albert (Elliot Burch), Stephen McHattie (Gabriel), Bill Marcus (D.A. Moreno), Richard Roundtree (Cleon Manning), Scott Wilkinson (Burton Fitch), Stanley Kamel (George Walker), Patrick St. Esprit (Arvin Cates)

Vincent reveals himself to Elliot Burch to get his aid in the search for Gabriel in "Nevermore," while Diana continues her own investigation.

P.K. Simonds notes, "I really liked writing the episode and the way it turned out, although I hated it when they first gave it to me. That was an episode that was very much in between other episodes and nothing monumental happened. But it was fun, because it had a noir quality to it and it brought Vincent to interesting places. It was great to have that moment when Elliot gets to see who his competition was. You see that both of them are really making immense sacrifices in their lives for their love of Catherine, which really redeems Elliot in a lot of ways and makes him into a real hero. It also allows two very unlikely friends to bond. Sometimes when you're writing something and you're not really sure what it's about, it forces you to dig a little deeper. You find interesting things and that process of discovery was the most rewarding part of the script."

"It pushed the story forward in a narratively taut way," Howard Gordon says, "and I think Elliot really came through for us as a character, and all these incidental characters sort of came to the fore. It was sort of a slow-moving meditation on loss and everything. There was the need for a mourning episode, and 'Nevermore' picked up the string. Basically, it was a revenge and rescue cycle set in motion. Vincent had a child to rescue, it was a quest, and there was an incredible emotional resonance."

Alex Gansa interjects, "It brought Elliot Burch into the fold and certainly spoke to his own reactions to Catherine's death and what was going on. Obviously it was an episode where he meets Vincent, which is certainly exciting on that level."

Notes Victor Lobl, "That was the first time I did any real work with Edward Albert. For me, it's always terrific to start work with another actor and Ed's real intense about getting it right, so he brought a lot of fresh energy to the set. It was also interesting to do something where Vincent was actually physically vulnerable, and it was new territory to travel with Ron. That's always liberating to have new places to go with an actor that you've been working with for a couple of years.

"What was interesting is what we came to in terms of trying to get a handle on that premise. Vincent and Elliot were both facets of the same personality in some ways. Elliot was somebody who had totally remade himself into this kind of mogul. He worked his way from the street and has this very slick façade that he started to throw away, because basically he was a street fighter. When it came down to it, that's the way he was going to deal with adversity. As he became more animal, it drew him closer to Vincent, who was actually extremely civilized, but also, in essence, was a street fighter. The way the two actors worked together was trying to find this thing in each other and trying to see each other, in some ways, as a reflection of themselves. That's the handle we looked at in all their scenes together."

Episode 3.5
"Snow"
Original Airdate: December 27, 1989
Written by George R.R. Martin
Directed by Gus Trikonis
Guest Starring: Stephen McHattie (Gabriel), Laurel Moglen (Brooke), Lance Henriksen (Snow), Randy Kaplan (Stephen), Lewis Smith (Mark)

Lance Henriksen portrays "Snow," Gabrielle's brother in arms, the two of them symbolically united by a pair of 500-year-old rings. In the episode, Snow goes Below to kill Vincent and just about anything else that moves.

"It was not my idea," says George R.R. Martin. "Steve Kurzfeld had this notion of Gabriel sending a killer into the tunnels. The real kind of action piece in the tunnels. Originally, Howard and Alex were going to write it, because I had reworked the Land of the Dead Trilogy. I had it boiled down to one episode called 'Where No Birds Sing,' which was supposed to follow the funeral episode, 'Walk Slowly.' It would be Vincent going to Narcissa and then going into the Land of the Dead searching for Catherine, but ultimately hearing his child's voice and essentially choosing life over death and Catherine. In fact, I had the outline for that and was about to write the teleplay, when Tony Thomas — who was more in the realistic camp — called me. He felt that the episode was too backward looking, too fantasy-oriented, and we couldn't do it. Because the third season was an arc, I couldn't just think of something I wanted to write, so assignments sort of got switched around and I got the 'Snow' episode, which was fun to do in a lot of ways.

"My assignment was to do a relentless action piece. It's a very violent episode, which I know bothers the fans, but that's what I set out to do. My belief about violence is that if it is going to happen, I wanted to affect people. That's why I'm proud of the way that I think *Beauty and the Beast* handled violence in general, through all of our seasons. Throughout television, violence is so clean. Somebody gets shot, and they fall down and they're never anybody you care about. *Murder, She Wrote* comes on every week and there's a body every week. Have you ever seen a moment of grief? Television robs violence and death of its emotional content.

"If 'Snow' was scary, if 'Snow' hurt people, if it was devastating to kill Steven and Sam and see this guy unleashed in the tunnels, if it was a sense of violation the way he smashed through the tunnel door — all of which some of the fans were upset by — my response is, 'Good. That's what I *wanted* to do.' I don't want to kill someone and have people say nothing. If I'm going to portray death in my fiction or my television, I want to provoke an emotional response. Death *should* provoke an emotional response.

"In 'Snow' we also started to get into the mystery of the rings, which I guess is going to remain one of the great unsolved secrets of *Beauty and the*

Beast, because we weren't finished with them. At the end of 'Invictus,' you don't know all there is to know about these rings. We know that Gabriel had one and Snow had the other, that they're 500 years old, that they have a Latin inscription... you find out some of this, but the whole story hasn't been told, because we didn't know we were going to be cancelled. We were talking about introducing a third ring and bringing in a third villain who had it. There was much more to deal with in another trilogy."

Howard Gordon admits, "I was skeptical about it, and I thought some of the metaphors were a little heavy-handed, like Vincent having these snow dreams. Ultimately, I think it worked, largely on the charisma of Lance Henriksen. I think he was a formidable opponent, and an apt emissary for Gabriel. We also had this intimation of their past, that they'd done terrible deeds together and that he was basically the best there was. I thought it was an effective, suspenseful hour of TV. We did, however, have quite a number of fights on staff about the violence, because things were fairly grim to begin with. On the one hand, it established the ruthlessness of the guy, but on the other, it left people with a very bad taste in their mouth. It did serve to make his own demise much sweeter."

Laughs Alex Gansa, "At some level, it introduced Vincent's precognition. I just remember George arguing against precognition in the first season episode 'Down to a Sunless Sea' as a horrible device, and then to use it in such a ludicrous fashion in 'Snow'... Give me a break, George. I love George, but I will never, ever let him live this one down. Dreaming of a blizzard in the tunnels all because there's a character named snow on the way down there. That's incredibly far-fetched. Anyway, there was some good stuff between Snow and Gabriel, and ultimately good cat and mouse down in the tunnels with Vincent. It was an extremely exciting action episode. You can't ask for better. That was our mandate, and that's what we gave, so we delivered on that show particularly."

Gus Trikonis reflects warmly on the episode. "When I read that show, I thought, 'This is terrific, a truly action-oriented film with character.' The guy who played Snow was wonderful, reminding me of Rutger Hauer in *Blade Runner*. The visual concepts were great, and so were the scenes between Lance Henriksen and Stephen McHattie.

"Remember Snow's red visor? The only way we could make that work was to have a light shining through it. It looked ominous, but he couldn't see through it. Every time he had that mask on, he was blind. When Lance was running through those tunnels, he didn't know where he was going. The only thing he could see was straight down at his feet, so there would be times when he would bump into walls. But you'd never know it from the way he handled it."

Episode 3.6
"Beggar's Comet"
Original Airdate: January 3, 1990
Written by George R.R. Martin
Directed by Victor Lobl
Guest Starring: Stephen McHattie (Gabriel), Edward Albert (Elliot Burch),
John Michael Golger (Greg Hughes), Laurel Moglen (Brooke), Stanley Kamel
(George Walker), Mike Jolly (Pierson), Nick LaTour (Clarence), John Lehne
(Jonathan Pope), Ben Piazza (Richards)

The financial collapse of Elliot Burch, orchestrated by Gabriel, takes place in "Beggar's Comet." Gabriel sways Elliot to his side, resulting in Burch's willingness to betray Vincent. At the last moment, though, he has a change of heart and sacrifices himself to save the man-beast. The episode concludes with an explosion that kills Elliot and seriously injures Vincent, who collapses on Catherine's grave.

"In the episode 'Nevermore,' Vincent goes to Elliot and it's a very dramatic meeting between these two men who both love Catherine," muses George R.R. Martin, "and he asks for Elliot's help. You have a great moment of drama there. But once you pass a moment of drama, you realize you've got a problem. Vincent, in some sense, has handed the baton to Elliot in a relay race and Elliot is in a position to do this investigating and find out stuff that Vincent can't. So, your central character in the drama doesn't have much to do, and he has to periodically go to Elliot and say, 'What's up this week?' I think some of this dictated the shape of 'Beggar's Comet.' I think we had to go in that direction to avoid becoming the Elliot Burch show. I do think we could have taken a little longer and that we could have gotten a few more beats out of Elliot's adoption of the trail, but it seemed to work pretty well."

Howard Gordon notes, "This was a failure on all of our parts to really deepen the Diana character. She was fine when she was a Manhunter, but I don't think we made her knowledge of Catherine intimate enough. She basically perused the scene of things, sniffed around and intimated rather than really investigated. There's just certain depth to Diana's character that I think we missed. Another mistake was the relationship with her boyfriend. She's got her own life. I think it was a mistake not to give more to that relationship. In an earlier draft, that relationship was supposed to be explored, but we ended up cutting it to a very incidental one.

"A thing I like about 'Beggar's Comet' is the last minute when Elliot's soul really redeemed itself. That idea I liked very much. The whole arc really included Elliot's really being humbled by Gabriel. He was a titan, the guy we had set up as the Prince of New York, and Gabriel was making mincemeat out of him."

"Beggar's Comet" marked Victor Lobl's final episode of *Beauty and the Beast*, though "In the Forest of the Night" would air after this one. "To me, it was particularly poignant," he says, "because I was saying goodbye to the entire experience after three years. It's one of those situations where you're shooting and shooting and you almost don't want to be on schedule. You want to fall behind and stretch it out as long as you can. The last night, we were shooting in the graveyard trying to beat the sunrise, and it was the scene between Gabriel and Elliot, two very strong actors given very strong material to work with. It was one of those production highs that I get occasionally that we don't know if we're going to get it and everybody's juiced up to try and do it, and we just kind of squeaked in under the wire and got it done.

"As I've said, I was not particularly thrilled with some of these scripts, partly because of where we had come from. If I had come to *Beauty and the Beast* in the third season, I would have approached it very differently, because my expectations would be different. But because it drifted away from what it had been, I felt a loss of the original concept so that I never engaged the material quite as much as I had in the prior years. But I think most of the work we did fulfilled the material as written."

Episode 3.7
"A Time to Heal"
Original Airdate: January 10, 1990
Written by Alex Gansa & Howard Gordon
Directed by Gus Trikonis
Guest Starring: Ellen Geer (Mary), Laurel Moglen (Brooke), Lewis Smith (Mark), Daniel Faraldo (Jorge)

At the beginning of "A Time to Heal," Diana finds Vincent on Catherine's grave and brings him back to her loft to begin the healing process.

"This was an exact reversal of Vincent bringing Catherine back to health," notes Alex Gansa. "This is the woman, now, healing the beast, which establishes some sort of connection between them. Ultimately, though, another very slow moving, dramatically insufficient script and not one of our best. We just didn't have the spark between these two. We tried, but I just don't think it was ultimately successful in that way. It didn't do what it was supposed to do, which was to create a real romantic energy between our leads."

Says George R.R. Martin, "I could've done without the little bit of action at the end, where she goes into the tunnel that just happens to be full of drug addicts, and Vincent just happens to be there at that moment, which I tried to eliminate. I guess the feeling was that they needed some action or something."

"It was a tough time for Jo Anderson because she was just breaking into the show," notes Gus Trikonis. "At the time I was wondering why they hired her. She was *so* different. I thought she lacked the necessary sensuality, and kind of depth that I felt was needed for that part. She did soften eventually, but that was in the planning of the arc. I just thought by the time they brought her to that place, people had lost interest. It was too late. But Jo worked her ass off, and I think the episode worked beautifully. It was really two characters in a room going on and on. We really got to watch the development of these two people."

Howard Gordon opines, "Some great moments in it. Alex and I worked very hard on that one, because dramatically we wanted to reverse the pilot and the myth, in that beauty saves the beast. Having been hot on his trail and having sort of insinuated herself into the psychic depth of the relationship, she really rescues him from death and heals him, and knows him at some level. All of those factors are very interesting, whether it all came out on screen, I'm not sure. I think it at least established the possibility of this relationship, and her helping Vincent on this quest to regain the child."

Episode 3.8
"In the Forest of the Night"
Original Airdate: July 21, 1990*
Written by P.K. Simonds, Jr.
Directed by Victor Lobl
Guest Starring: Stephen McHattie (Gabriel), Tony Plana (Horner), Terrance Ellis (Rolley), Tony Colitti (Tony), Keeley Marie Gallagher (Alexandra), Suzie Plakson (Susan), Miguel Sandoval (Jerry)

"In the Forest of the Night" marks the return of Rolley, and Vincent's attack on the drug warehouse that belongs to Gabriel.

P.K. Simonds states, "I hated that episode from beginning to end. I was miserable, constantly arguing to drop the episode out and shorten the arc. In terms of its relationship to the arc, it had deep structural problems and the connection to Gabriel in that story was very tenuous. It was nice to bring back Rolley and explore his character a little more, offering a chance of redemption, but, again, it's all these people you don't care about. A show like *Beauty and the Beast* just doesn't do hard-bitten criminals very well. It's very difficult to combine the tones of our show and a show that depicts those kinds of characters realistically. It was depressing, violent, unpleasant and just didn't take us forward at all. I just thought it was a waste."

---

* *Note: Although this episode was intended to be aired during the arc, due to declining ratings and a firm cancellation date it was held back until a summer broadcast.*

"I think it's an important episode in the development of the relationship between Vincent and Diana," says George R.R. Martin.

Howard Gordon notes, "I rank this with 'Hollow Men,' not one of my favorite episodes. In the most cynical terms, it was a filler episode, although it did develop the Vincent/Diana relationship. But not a great episode."

"The storyline of this script was very shaky," recalls Victor Lobl. "We had a lot of problems making the logic of it work. The whole time I was shooting *Beauty and the Beast*, this was the first episode I worked on that had many gaps in continuity and logic, and everything was so heavily under the gun that there was a fear of unraveling the entire script while trying to solve some of the fundamental flaws in it. It became a kind of battleground for everybody. Not an angry battleground, but there were real opposing views about how far we should try to solve some of these problems, and how many we should simply let go and not worry about. Just in terms of action, there was some pretty exciting stuff, but the part of the script that dealt with Rolley was not sufficiently explored. It seemed to me a little thin. The action worked beautifully. The rest didn't."

Episode 3.9
"Chimes at Midnight"
Original Airdate: January 17, 1990
Written by Linda Campanelli & Shelly Moore
Directed by Ron Perlman
Guest Starring: Stephen McHattie (Gabriel), Terrance Ellis (Rolley), Tony Plana (Horner), Tom Donaldson (Nash), Leonard R. Garner, Jr. (Carlo), Steven Gilborn (Martin), Kenneth Kimmins (Doctor), John Lehne (Jonathan Pope), June Kyoto Lu (Tenko), Steve Mittleman (Sonny), Kathryn Spitz (Rebecca)

Vincent is captured by Gabriel, while simultaneously an empathic bond is established between Vincent and his son.

"Probably the least amount of dialogue in any episode of *Beauty and The Beast*," laughs Linda Campanelli, "because it was all Diana out at night trying to get away from the bad guys, and Vincent having this weird fantasy vision through the forest."

Howard Gordon states, "The connection between Vincent and his son was great, and Gabriel's obsession with the child and Vincent ultimately becomes his undoing. I felt McHattie was great here, and I think things began to congeal for us. Some of the fans hated the episode, because they just couldn't stand to see Vincent being imprisoned or hurt. It was clearly painful to some people, and that's not what the series was about. The series was really about this love, so we kind of changed the rules midstream for

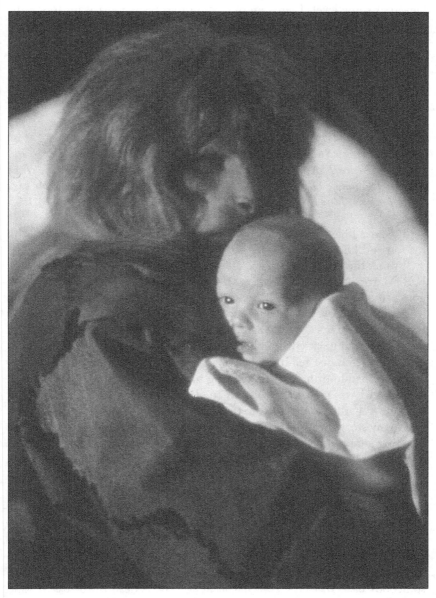

VINCENT WITH JACOB, HIS AND THE LATE CATHERINE CHANDLER'S SON.
(PHOTO: CBS).

a lot of people. Our logic was that they would get behind Vincent on this quest because it was avenging the loss of that love, but maybe our logic was flawed at some level. There's an old axiom that people just want to see the pilot again and again and again every week. That may be true."

Episode 3.10
"Invictus"
Original Airdate: January 24, 1990
Written by George R.R. Martin
Directed by Gus Trikonis
Guest Starring: Stephen McHattie (Gabriel), John Michael Bolger (Greg Hughes), Kenneth Kimmins (Doctor), John Lehne (Jonathan Pope), Tony Maggio (Sammy), Dayton Callie (Hitman), Alex Datcher (Andrea), Richard Feld (Janitor), June Kyoto Lu (Tenko)

The arc comes to a close with "Invictus," in which Vincent is united with his son and Diana kills Gabriel with a bullet from Catherine's gun.

"I think the key point of 'Invictus' was the death of Gabriel," says George R.R. Martin. "We wrestled with this for a long time. What the hell were we going to do with this guy? Is he going to get the baby and get away? Does he get killed? How are we going to make this dramatic? Does Vincent rip him to shreds? He's a great villain, but when you get up to him on a physical level, he's not a great villain. He's a guy in an Armani suit. The thing about Catherine's gun just fell into place marvelously. It just came to me one day and it seemed to bring the whole thing full circle symbolically and dramatically. And I was glad to go with it. In 'The Outsiders,' Catherine brought her gun to Father to protect the tunnels. I had really opposed that, and we had many story meetings where I opposed the whole concept of Catherine bringing a gun into the tunnels. Not because I was opposed to guns per se, but because I thought it was introduced too late structurally in the episode. Alex and Howard obviously felt different. They were doing the rewrite and prevailed in that particular struggle. In retrospect, I'm glad that they did.

"Stephen McHattie was very chlling. It's interesting to see the fans' reaction. They seem to love to hate Paracelsus, but they just hate Gabriel. They also claimed we were going too fast with the Vincent/Diana relationship. I frankly don't see how we could have gone any slower. We didn't want to do the thing, 'Well, Catherine's dead, next episode Vincent is in love with somebody else.' In fact, Catherine, although she is dead third season, kind of dominates the episodes. Her name comes up constantly, her presence is always there behind the scenes and the child exists as a living embodiment of the relationship between Catherine and Vincent. This whole thing was not a plot development that any of us would have chosen, but once Linda

STEPHEN MCHATTIE, WHO EPITOMIZED EVIL AS GABRIEL IN SEASON THREE (PHOTO: CBS).

made the decision to leave, we had to continue and I think the choices we made were valid. You can argue some of them, but unlike the first two seasons, the third season had high points and low points. Nonetheless, on the whole, I think it was successful."

"'Invictus' was great," enthuses Alex Gansa, "and the way the gun came back was fantastic. George told a great story. There were the typical contrivances, but I just thought that one was full of power. Again, the story was better on the page, but it turned out really well. Outstanding."

Howard Gordon muses, "I think George did a great, great job strictly on a storytelling level with having Diana pull the trigger. It's a morally ambiguous moment, legally. By killing this guy, it certainly made her a worthy prospective lover for Vincent. Her kind of no shit attitude and incredible pragmatism defined her character in a way. It was a kind of deepening that we needed to make for a worthy companion. A great culmination to an arc."

Adds Gus Trikonis, "'Invictus' was my best episode. I really peaked out in that show in terms of the visual power, the sense of control over my lenses, the movement of the camera, the actors' performances, the dynamics of the scenes and how they were going to be shot…all of those things. They just all came together for me in that show."

Episode 3.11
"The Reckoning"
Original Airdate: July 28, 1990
Written by Howard Gordon & Alex Gansa
Directed by Kenneth R. Koch

Episode 3.12
"Legacies"
Original Airdate: August 4, 1990
Written by Written by P.K. Simonds, Jr.
Directed by Gus Trikonis
Guest Starring: Ellen Geer (Mary), Ritch Brinkley (William), Terrylene (Laura Williams), Fionnula Flanagan (Jessica Webb), David Graf (Gregory Coyle), John Pleshette (Jimmy Faber), Jeff Corey (Winston Burke), Elayne Heilveil (Olivia), Patrick Y. Malone (Darryl), Vachik Mangassarian (Lewis Windham), Patricia Place (Deborah), Kathryn Spitz (Rebecca), Teddy Wilson (Raymond Ensign), Delane Vaughn (Young Raymond), Lauren White (Dr. Nyhart)

The series concluded with the two-part "The Reckoning" and "Legacies," tracing the serial killings of a former tunnel dweller. Concurrently, Vincent's son, named Jacob, is brought to the world Below.

Of these episodes, Howard Gordon explains, "The thought behind the scenes was that we would show where the show could go, explore the status of the relationship between Vincent and Diana and where it's going. This was the time to sort of lay all that out and reestablish the franchise. A fairly conventional idea was a serial murderer. Also, there had been other stories on the back burner, like Father falling in love again. The genesis of the two-parter was that we felt pushing the story of the underworld forward was a way of moving the series forward — really confronting the issues of Father passing on or at least passing the mantle on to Vincent."

"As far as I'm concerned," adds Alex Gansa, "I wish those things had never seen the light of day, and when they were written, I never expected them to see the light of day. First of all, Howard and I had a weekend to write the story for both shows. We had no time to do it, we were under tremendous pressure and we never really thought the shows would air, because we were already cancelled. Ultimately we didn't have a very interesting villain or a very interesting plot. The one good thing was Father and this woman from his life. That and the material with the baby was fine, but the serial murderer...God!"

"A frustrating show in some ways," admits P.K. Simonds, "because it was, again, not something I was excited about writing. There were some interesting things about the history of the tunnels and Gregory's story, but I hated the serial killer thing. We did toy around with some different endings which were more suggestive about Diana's feelings for Vincent. I think we ultimately backed away from doing anything that was too pointedly romantic between them, and I thought that was a mistake. My feeling was that we should shit or get off the pot with their romance, and they kept making me get off the pot."

George R.R. Martin interjects, "I liked the Father love story, but the whole serial killer plot was a bad idea. I'm sorry we did that. Howard Gordon did not want to do that. He strongly argued for a couple of joyful episodes. You know, 'The crisis is over, let's have some fun now. Let's have the naming ceremony, Father falling in love, let's do a pure character piece.' It was largely Steven Kurzfeld and I guess Paul and Tony who wanted to continue with the action and all that. Gabriel's dead, let's get another lunatic in there. Let's kill some more people. I don't think it worked. Unlike Gabriel, the villain was not that threatening and the episodes not that suspenseful. The whole serial killer plotline just sort of sat there."

"Very episodic," sighs "Legacies" director Gus Trikonish. "In general, the show itself didn't offer much."

As the writing staff did their best to work through the third season, the fans were in an uproar and made sure that the writers were well aware of their dissatisfaction. "That was a real painful experience," admits Howard Gordon. "When they turn on you, they really turn on you. People, whose attention and adoration of the show was pretty serious, took a spurned lover kind of approach. It was painful for all of us. The letters, the phone calls, the attitude people had taken was that it was their show, and we had killed it or ruined it. You try not to take it seriously and treat it as a handful of excessive fans, but it still hurt, and we felt sorry for doing it."

P.K. Simonds notes, "My car was vandalized in such a way that I'm fairly certain it was an angry fan who did it."

Alex Gansa says, "It was unbelievable. I was getting calls on my machine, and I don't know how they got my home number. They were just being extremely vitriolic on the phone, yelling and cursing. Just horrible stuff.

"Whether or not the third season was a success… personally, I did not think so. I didn't think it worked for a lot of reasons. One, I think this whole notion of a super villain was a bum steer from the beginning. Largely what happened was that everybody in the writing team lent some quality to Gabriel. Someone wanted him to be a major businessman, another person wanted him to be a latter date Ninja/kung fu warrior, somebody else wanted him to be a mercenary, somebody else wanted him to have some strange psychic connection with Vincent. When you finally piled all of these qualities and characteristics into one person, he became kind of a joke.

"Now, Stephen McHattie did a fantastic job. He is a wonderful actor and thank God we were able to get him. But on the level of super villain, I thought it left a lot to be desired. I also thought the whole idea of introducing a second beauty into Vincent's life was a dicey prospect at best. Imbuing either of them with any feeling for each other was going to be tricky. I don't think we ever solved it or began to solve it in the first half of the season, and I thought if the show had continued we would have had a hell of a time doing it. We were also losing the fans that had stuck with the show for romance, and we weren't gaining any of the men who wanted action. In the third season, we moved away from the strengths of the show, which was romance, because somebody, including us, mistakenly thought that what people wanted to see was a much more plot-driven, action-oriented show. Once Linda left, we were doomed anyway. I truly believe that if Linda had stayed with the show, we would have stayed on the air. Nonetheless, I applaud the creative chance we took. With our hands tied behind her back and her feet tied together, we were still able to jump around a couple of steps."

Howard Gordon offers, "I think that whole third season was a very noble experiment, although I'm not sure that it worked. There was a bittersweet quality to the whole thing, because there was so much negative stuff going on with the fans and it was reflected in the ratings. It wasn't fun to be on a sinking ship. On the other hand, the fighter in us definitely wanted to make it work, to resurrect it and go forward. What upset me is that the third season was a false start in that we had to find a new beauty, and we never did really get to find her. So, in a sense, we kind of began an experiment and didn't follow it through."

George Martin is, frankly, confused by all the outcry. "I've read letters from fans who said everything was different third season," he shakes his head. "Really, the only thing different was Catherine. Other than that, it was the same writers, the same directors, the same actors, the same set, the same cinematographer, all trying very hard to create some sense of continuity or the same mood. Of course, we had to take realism into account. With Vincent grieving, we couldn't do light episodes and we couldn't have much romance when we had killed the female lead, although it was always planned to get back to it eventually. We were just doing it slowly. Recasting Catherine, I think, would have produced a failure just as quickly, but a less interesting one."

Reflecting on the show's demise, Howard Gordon says, "You always try to look at the bright side and be positive about things. I convinced myself I was ready to move on, but it was definitely a mourning period. The show had really become a part of us all, and it was really hard to leave. It was a great experience to be part of a show that was considered that special by so many people. When David Letterman, Johnny Carson and *Saturday Night Live* bring you up on their shows, you know you've infiltrated the collective consciousness. Most shows don't get to do that. TV is really populated with a lot of mediocre stuff, and here was something that really reached for excellence."

In wrapping up his comments on the show, George Martin reflects warmly on the opportunity provided to him and the other writers by Ron Koslow. "I think all television shows need someone in charge of the writing staff who has a strong vision and is powerful enough to convey that vision to the other writers," he says. "If you don't have that, then you get into the problem of everybody going off in different and sometimes contradictory directions. On the other hand, if you have someone who is too strong, who's a dictator and doesn't allow you to go in different directions, then you have a staff of typists who are taking dictations from one person. If I had not been allowed to create characters like Mouse or things like the Whispering Gallery as well as directions I had developed, I would not have stayed on the show for a lengthy period of time. It was those aspects of the job and the fact that Ron Koslow gave us freedom that made the job so fulfilling. Much more fulfilling than the average television show where everything is locked in concrete.

"I was sorry the show ended. I wanted it to go on and if it had, I was going to be co-executive producer with Steve Kurzfeld, so it was a little frustrating for me personally. I had another dozen stories that I was dying to tell. I had plots and ideas and directions to take the show that were just waiting to happen."

States Gus Trikonis, "Ron Koslow said to me at the beginning of the season, 'What we're trying to do is turn the ship around going down the river and I don't know if we're going to.' Well, they didn't quite make it, but, God, did they work hard trying to get it around."

Admitted Ron Perlman, "It's difficult to take a show that is so fundamentally *about* something and make a sharp left turn like they did, and it's no one's fault, it's just the way circumstances happened to fall. Now, I'm not a big fan of reading demographics and whether our ratings in fact actually seemed to erode after Catherine died, but we were asking an awful lot of people who had invested a great deal of themselves in the story of these two lovers to perhaps go down a path that they weren't readily accepting of, and we were such a borderline show with regard to the way CBS viewed us all along that any move we made teetering in any direction would have caused our demise, and I think basically that's what happened.

"I was as curious as everyone else as to what they were going to do in season three and we learned it as we were going along. Ron and the writers sat up there in their ivory towers and brainstormed and figured. You'd only get a script like two or three days before you were getting ready to film it, because you were so busy working on the script that was being filmed at the moment. As a result, I didn't have the chance to ponder whether I liked it or not, and my job was to just do it and do it as well as possible and let the chips fall where they may. I do acknowledge the fact that it's very, very tough to change the course of a show that is built so strongly on the presence of two characters, and to put the burden on another one and reintroduce a third is asking a lot. I think that the wisdom behind that was that this show asked a lot from the get-go and, what the hey, try it and if it works, it works. If it doesn't work, it doesn't. I'm proud of some of the work that went into those last 11 episodes, they had some great things in them, but I understand the difficulties and we weathered a change of management at CBS when the new guy came in and said, 'You're outta here!'"

Closes *Beauty and the Beast* creator Ron Koslow, "I don't think there are too many television shows that have had to recreate themselves after two seasons. It was definitely an interesting exercise, and I definitely think we got a chance to explore things we ordinarily wouldn't have been able to. But then, I think all three seasons were adventures, and really admirable attempts considering that this was a show that by all the laws of television shouldn't have gone past the pilot. Everything was an experimentation and we tried different things. Sometimes it worked and sometimes it didn't, and when you're experimenting, you have to have the freedom to fail. But when it worked, I think it approached a depth of feeling on television that maybe hasn't been felt before."

THE UNSEEN *BEAUTY*
AND THE BEAST

Through the course of every television series, there are numerous teleplays or treatments which are developed but never make it to the air. Sometimes this is attributed to the quality of said storyline, which may not be up to par with the rest of the series, while at other times it has nothing to do with the quality of the tale whatsoever. Perhaps there are political motivations behind such decisions, or what was written would have far exceeded the allotted budget for an hourly episode. Maybe the series has changed creative directions and what might have been appropriate at one time, no longer fits. Whatever the reason, locked in the vaults of every production studio are numerous stories which were purchased and never taken any farther.

What follows is an August 12, 1988 story break-down for what would have been the episodes for the show's second season. It's interesting to note which episodes remained and which were discarded when the show changed dramatic course.

1. "The Young Knight," *by P.K. Simonds*
Vincent asks Catherine to help a beautiful young man from the tunnels in his transition to the world above. As her relationship with the young prodigy of Vincent develops, she finds herself attracted to all the qualities that remind her of Vincent. *(This episode eventually aired as "A Fair and Perfect Knight.")*

2. "Plague," *by Roy Dotrice and Durrel Royce Crays*
Catherine and Vincent rescue a Russian sailor (Dimitri) who seeks asylum in order to be re-united with his true love...As Catherine searches for Dimitri's lover, he becomes seriously ill...Father quickly realizes that Dimitri has cholera and he must lead the community out of this crisis. *(Eventually retitled "Ashes, Ashes".)*

3. "Vincent's It's a Wonderful Life," *by Virginia Aldridge.*

Blinded by his desire to salvage the soul of Joshua, an emotionally disturbed child who has turned to Vincent to be his father, Vincent refuses to follow the advice of Father and Catherine; he cannot bring himself to turn Joshua over to Catherine so he can receive professional help. Joshua slips into a violent self-destructive rage, endangering all and culminating in his death. Devastated by this loss, Vincent can only see the pain that he has brought to all those he has ever loved. Reeling with self-doubt, Vincent rushes to the abyss to end his life…Here, he is confronted by an angel who appears in Catherine's form and guides him through a tour of the lives of his loved ones so that he can view them as they would be if he had never entered their lives. *(Although this episode eventually reached the air as "Remember Love," the motivation for Vincent's depression was not as strong. In the final version, he's upset by the fact that he and Catherine can't do something as simple as going camping together. Not quite the emotional depth as originally conceived.)*

4. "Chamber Music," *by Ron Koslow*

As he roams the city, Vincent encounters a ravaged young junkie who was once a gifted child musician in the tunnels. With Catherine's help he tries to find the young man and bring him back. *(This episode opened the second season.)*

5. "Mary Magdalene (X-Mas Story)," *by Alex Gansa and Howard Gordon*

With Catherine's help, a pregnant hooker determined to get her life on the straight track is granted refuge in the tunnel world. There, she enjoys the compassion and support she has never known. Buoyed by the miracle of new life and the reawakening of her hope, she begins to thrive…and to fall deeply in love with Vincent. On Christmas Day, she gives birth to a baby girl and she wants Vincent to be the child's father. In the course of the episode, Father will tell the story of how Vincent was found. *(Retitled "God Bless the Child.")*

6. "Mitch," *by David Peckinpah*

Sam Denton becomes fatally ill; he appeals to Vincent to bring Mitch to him so that they can be reconciled…Vincent must convince Catherine and Father that Sam's last wish be honored. Mitch betrays Vincent by attempting to escape through the tunnels. Ultimately, Mitch proves that Vincent's faith in him is justified when he chooses to spare Vincent and Catherine. He surrenders and returns to prison. *(Originally called "The Prodigal" and never produced. Full synopsis follows.)*

7. "Winterfest," *by George R.R. Martin*

Each year the community gathers to honor the network of helpers with a grand feast and celebration. Paracelsus uses the occasion to smuggle an agent disguised as a helper into the world below to murder Father or Vincent. *(Retitled "Dead of Winter," and it was Paracelsus himself who invaded Winterfest.)*

8. "Orphans," *by Alex Gansa and Howard Gordon*

After a long battle with cancer, Catherine's father finally succumbs. Before his death, Catherine brings Vincent to meet her father. The loss profoundly affects Catherine, and her depression forces her to take a leave of absence from work. Feeling totally disconnected from anyone or thing in the above world — her psychiatrist provides little solace — she finds sanctuary in the tunnel world. Vincent and Father and the entire community join together to help her heal and come to terms with her orphaned state. In the end, Catherine's reluctance to return to her life is something that must be resolved for her to become whole again.

9. "Sticks and Stones," *by Alex Gansa and Howard Gordon*

Catherine discovers Laura's involvement with a violent gang of deaf kids, and with the undercover cop who has infiltrated the gang.

10. "Isaac's High Noon," *by David Peckinpah*

In avenging his sister's death from drugs, Isaac incurs the wrath of the neighborhood drug lord who sends his forces to kill Isaac. No one in the neighborhood will come to Isaac's aid and Vincent must intervene. *(An unfilmed episode.)*

11. "Brothers," *by George R.R. Martin*

Devin becomes involved with the "Dragonman," a deformed man, at a carnival when he learns that he is enslaved by his brother, forced to endure life as a sideshow freak. Devin helps the Dragonman to escape and brings him to the world below.

12. "The Return of Elliot Burch," *by David Peckinpah*

Still obsessed with Catherine, Elliot hires a private detective to discover the identity of Catherine's lover and learns of Vincent and the world below. *(An unfilmed episode.)*

13. "The Abyss," *by Ron Koslow*

A brutal heavy metal street gang invades the tunnels, killing and terrorizing the tunnel people. Vincent's life becomes a pitched battle as he fights to protect his world. After rescuing Catherine from their grip, the siege culminates in a hand to hand battle between Vincent and the vicious leader of the gang on a footbridge over the abyss. *(A variation of this episode aired as "The Outsiders." The final battle as described sounds similar to the one between Vincent and Jason Walker in season one's "Terrible Savior.")*

14. "Toxic Waste," *author unknown*

Toxic wastes are being dumped into the tunnels. Several of the children become ill. Catherine must find the culprits before the tunnel world becomes uninhabitable, but without exposing its existence. *(An unfilmed episode.)*

15. "The Darkest Night," *by Ron Koslow*

Vincent tells the story of the darkest night of his life which led him to Central Park where he found Catherine as she lay dying. *(Unfilmed, but what a great episode this would have made.)*

16. "Triangle," *by David Peckinpah*

Jamie falls for an attractive topsider and turns to Catherine for advice and support as she pursues this "secret love." Meanwhile, Mouse confesses his love for Jamie to Vincent with the hope that Vincent will help him become Jamie's ideal suitor. Ultimately, Jamie learns that the love she sought above was already present below; Mouse learns that the only way to win Jamie's love is to be true to himself. *(Although this would have given secondary characters a chance to shine, the storyline was dropped. Interestingly, the "love being where you least expect it" theme was used in season three's climactic two-parter, "Legacies" and "The Reckoning," the characters involved being Father and Mary.)*

17. "Sunset, Sunrise," *by Ron Koslow*

Catherine wants to show Vincent the sunrise and sunset at a magical place of her childhood, a mountain lake. Their adventure begins as a quest to spirit Vincent out of the city, but becomes a nightmare. Yet at the sight of the sunrise, they both agree it was worth it. *(Part of this storyline was worked into "Remember Love.")*

18. "A Tale Told," *by Linda Campanelli and M.M. Shelly Moore*

Catherine comes down with a bad case of the flu and must stay home to recover. Vincent visits and when he asks Catherine if she would like him to read to her, she tells him she would prefer it if he made up a story. As Vincent tells the tale, Catherine envisions herself and Vincent as the heroine and hero of his story. And when Vincent completes his story with an unsatisfactory conclusion, Catherine insists that he provide the happy ending she knows they both desire. *(Great concept. Too bad it never went beyond the story stage.)*

19. "Father Relives His Betrayal," *by Alex Gansa and Howard Gordon*

Father is called above to fulfill an important mission and finds himself confronting the scientist who betrayed him during the HUAC hearings. *(Unfilmed. An interesting sequel of sorts to season one's "Song of Orpheus.")*

20. "The Return of Elliot Burch," *by George R.R. Martin*

Cullen's artistry is fulfilled when Catherine arranges for him to have an exhibit of his works. Elliot Burch attends the exhibit and cannot comprehend how Cullen (who he takes to be Catherine's secret lover) was able to win Catherine's heart. Unable to find out anything about Cullen's background, he hires a private detective to determine who he is and where he comes from. *(A variation of David Peckinpah's story of the same name, which was discussed earlier.)*

21. "The Wishing Well," *by Virginia Aldridge*

There is a wishing well in Central Park that empties into the tunnels. When the children hear an older gentleman make a wish to be reunited with his true love, they tell Vincent (who) enlists Catherine and together they are able to reunite the lovers. *(Unfilmed, probably due to the shift to more action oriented stories in the middle of the second season.)*

22. "The Blind Date," *by Paul Lance*

As a favor to Joe, Catherine agrees to go on a blind date with his heartbroken cousin. During the course of the evening, the blind date will get a glimpse of Catherine's "secret life." We will view her life from the blind date's point of view. *(An unfilmed episode.)*

23. "Time of Madness," *by Larry Carroll and David Carreno*

Many years ago, Vincent endured an horrific episode in which he lost control of his beastial side. Now that same madness has returned and it is worse than before. Believing that he will never regain control, Vincent says good-bye to all his loved ones and retreats to the deepest tunnels to die. *(Unfilmed, but aspects of this story most definitely made themselves known in the trilogy that wrapped up season two.)*

24. "Crime of Passion," *by Jeffrey Stepakoff*

Brooke, a young woman from below, falls in love with a topsider. Vincent and Catherine serve as go-between and bring the two lovers together. Unfortunately, a young man from the tunnels who has grown up with Brooke and has always loved her, is devastated by Brooke's new love and refuses to accept it. When it becomes apparent that Brooke has chosen to leave the world below to be with her lover, the spurned man murders his rival. The world below conducts a murder "trial" in which it is decided that the murderer is to be banished from their world. *(Unfilmed. Full synopsis follows.)*

25. "And Miles to Go Before I Sleep," *by George R.R. Martin*

Vincent tells the children the story of his Halloween evening out with Catherine. *(Unfilmed. One assumes that this would have been the show's second Halloween episode, but was abandoned when the 1988 Writer's Strike prevented them from getting the show on the air in time for the holiday.)*

INDEX

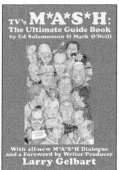

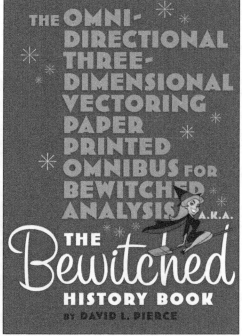
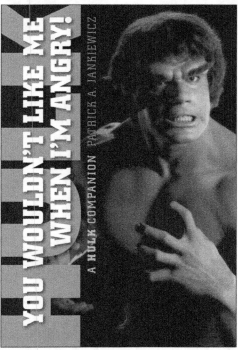

CPSIA information can be obtained at www.ICGtesting.com
Printed in the USA
LVOW04s0339260215

428421LV00003B/219/P

9 781593 932800